There's Something With Mr Neary

Mark Neary

Acknowledgements

To VJ, The H Man, Jayne & Shelley for giving me love, belief and balls

(Though not necessarily in that order)

Introduction

I wrote Get Steven Home in 2011 and the response was phenomenal. It still knocks me sideways when I hear that the book is essential reading on several social work courses. My motives at the time of writing the first book were pretty selfish; they were trying to make up for 35 years. When I started my A Levels, my plan was to go to university and study English and Politics and then hopefully get a job in journalism. Then at 16 my mother died and I told myself that my place was at home. It took three and a half decades to finally get something in print but the impact has been so rewarding.

In 2012, I started to write a blog about my experiences in the middle of the adult social care world (or as a friend put it; "on the receiving end of the social care world"). After the Neary vs Hillingdon court case in 2011, I naively expected life to be a bit easier. Sadly, the social care world is so complicated and at times, so hostile, that life is just as stressful as it ever was. I've come to the conclusion that social care isn't geared at all to the people it is meant to serve; we are an annoying inconvenience. It would be just wonderful to be able to walk away from the system but having a disabled person in the family makes that impossible. Every encounter I have with social services is a massive learning experience and I hope this book includes a few tips on how to navigate the system.

Basically this book is a collection of my blog writing with some extra bits thrown in for good measure. It's like one of those double CDs you can get with the greatest hits on side one and obscure b sides on the other side. I have made a clumsy attempt to collect the stories together under specific themes. But the over-riding theme is that the social care world is a very tough world to be part of. Caring for a disabled son is an absolute piece of piss when compared to attending multi disciplinary meetings; trying to decode the strange language endemic in the system; or having to manage a care package when all you really want to do is flop on the sofa with The Expendables. I hope there are some funny bits in the book because it is the dark side of social care that keeps me sane. I know I get angry at times, and there are some whingy parts to the book but my honest aim with the writing is to present my account of my life as a carer.

Paragraphs 56 & 57 of Justice Peter Jackson's judgement in Neary vs Hillingdon:

Regrettably, once Mr Neary's initial resistance to its plans weakened and fell away, Hillingdon appears to have taken a dim view of his concerns. In an e-mail dated 22 February from the social worker to the support unit, the following appears: *"There is always going to be something or other that Mr Neary will bring up and more often than not we are having to appease his needs rather than Steven's, however I want Steven to remain at [the support unit]. I know that it seems that you as a team are constantly being questioned but this will be the case because Mr Neary wants to find issues with the care that other people give Steven. We just need to ensure like we have that we are working together for the best outcome for Steven."*

It is now accepted by Hillingdon that Mr Neary had done nothing to deserve this disrespect. The unfortunate tone of the message demonstrates that even at this stage the expression *"working together"* did not include working together with Steven's father in the true sense and that Hillingdon's thinking had by this stage become adversarial. Worse, the professional view was withheld from Mr Neary, perhaps because revealing it would have provoked a renewed challenge. In the meantime, a "transition plan", ostensibly leading towards a return home, was put into place. It started on 4 March, with four phases: (1) 4/6 weeks of return home on Monday afternoons, (2) 4/6 weeks of return home on Monday and Tuesday afternoons, (3) the above plus Saturday afternoons at home, (4) the above plus a couple of overnight stays before a final return home. It was not until 8 July, by which time the four phases had been successfully accomplished, that Hillingdon told Mr Neary that it was not willing to return Steven to his care.

Personalisation   Resource Allocation Systems   Inclusion   Choice

Transition Management   Mental Capacity   Circles of Support

Hubs Positive Behaviour Support   Stakeholder Options   Carers

Risk Assessments   Fairer Charging Policy   Change Champions

Deprivation of Liberty Safeguards   Indicative Budgets   Flexibility

Empowerment   Directly Commissioned Services Best Interests

Person Centred Plans   Fairer Access to Services   Transformation

Continuing Care Assessments   Indicative Budgets   Inclusion

Hubs   Personalised Services   Panel   Transport Access

Direct Payments   Equitable Services   Challenging Behaviour

Service User   The Care Market   START Recording Analysis

Risk Management Plans   Circles of Support   Best Interests

Accessing the Community   Independent Living Transformers

Individual Budgets   Resource Allocation Systems   Choice

Core Needs   Fairer Access to Services   Service Brokerage

Personalisation   Resource Allocation Systems   Inclusion   Choice

Transition Management   Mental Capacity   Circles of Support

Hubs Positive Behaviour Support   Stakeholder Options   Carers

Risk Assessments   Fairer Charging Policy   Change Champions

Deprivation of Liberty Safeguards   Indicative Budgets   Flexibility

Empowerment   Directly Commissioned Services Best Interests

Person Centred Plans   Fairer Access to Services   Transformation

Continuing Care Assessments   Indicative Budgets   Inclusion

Life Since 2011

I look across at Steven sometimes, when he's sitting on the sofa, totally engrossed in one of his many Abba DVDS and experience a strange mixture of love, pride, anger and sadness. It was the love that kept me going during 2010. I'm proud of him for surviving such an appalling experience and although there are plenty of scars, his instinct is still to trust people (I could learn a lot from him because my ability to trust professionals in his care has been severely dented). I'm proud of the way he is maturing into a good man. He pushes himself and takes on challenges that he might have shied away from before as a child. I'm angry because he's learned in the cruellest way possible that life is unpredictable and that you can lose everything you value at the drop of a hat (or the whim of a social worker). I'm angry that after everything he's been through, the council are still putting him through it. Despite, everything the judge said, the council still stick to their myth about who Steven is and how he functions. And I'm sad because I know what the future holds for him and it's not good. I don't believe I stopped Steven being whisked off to a care home in Wales; I believe I postponed it.

But he's in a place now where people value his need for routines and although, it can be arse numbingly boring at times, it's something we do because it helps him feel safe. And if he feels safe, he is less likely to have a meltdown.

My life has changed dramatically since 2011. Following the court judgement and the publication of the book, I suddenly found myself being invited to speak at all manner of events and conferences. I was invited to join a panel on Radio 4 to discuss the state of the care industry in the UK; I have been asked to speak at legal conferences and on an almost monthly basis now, I get to address best interests' assessors and mental health advocates at events across the country. I was nominated for a Liberty Human Rights award and had a fabulous evening at the Royal festival Hall and met so many inspirational people. I've written for The Independent and for the Mind Newsletter and have guest blogged for other people's blogs. I took part in the filming of a promotional film for the company who supplied Steven with his IMCA during the court case. And it goes on: next month I've been invited to join a group at the House of Lords looking into an Independent Living Act. It's all been very exciting.

Last June, I also went out on my own with my own counselling practice. It's funny because the court considered the adverse effect of the publicity on Steven and they did have concerns about it. I can honestly say that for Steven, there hasn't been any negative experience arising from the press and media attention. However, I think it indirectly cause problems for me in my old workplace. I work as a counsellor and the attitude at the agency is rigidly psychodynamic – the counsellor is a blank screen and reveals nothing of themself. That was tricky as I was appearing on the front pages of the national press. Even though, I don't think it was a problem for a single one of my clients, it caused a lot of tension with the senior managers and after 14 years, it felt like time to leave. It has definitely been for the best and I now work in the most beautiful surroundings you can imagine.

But when you're trapped in the social care system, there is always something or other going on. As I write, Steven and I face the prospect of becoming homeless in the summer as a result of Hillingdon suddenly reinterpreting the Housing Benefit regulations and by having a very rigid housing allocation policy. It will probably all end up in court once again. I know though, that even when that is sorted, there will be another battle ahead. Steven had just been through the RAS and I suspect from a hint by the social worker that he is going to lose out big time. And as we try to get our heads round how we will manage on a much reduced support package, the next cab off the rank will be the fairer charging policy and Steven is likely to receive a heavy charge for his reduced service. It goes on and on. I know from the many comments and stories that appear on the Get Steven Home Facebook group that for most people, their biggest struggle isn't coping with their disabled family member but with the system that presents itself as the support. Crazy world.

Back to home. My favourite times are the evenings. Apart from my late night at work on Wednesdays, each evening it is just Steven and me on our own from 6 o'clock. It's great having the support team but it can feel intrusive at times. As I write this, Steven has been back home 838 days and I haven't once had to deal with any behaviour that I cannot manage. In court, Hillingdon presented a picture that I was at grave risk when I'm on my own and to deal with the risk, I force feed Steven Mars bars. Now that the spotlight is off me, the whole idea is laughable. It is in the evenings that Steven does most of his talking; I think that although he is fond of his support workers, he relaxes when it is just me and him. Last night, we had a two hour Beautiful South DVD session, whilst chatting about: Gene Kelly; The things that you don't get in Easter Eggs; his grandmother's leg bandage; who all the members of East 17 resemble from his schooldays; how many people we know called Des; what he's going to say when he sees his uncle next week; the problems of shitting in a ball pool; where our next door neighbour keeps his motorcycle helmet when he's eating his Rice Krispies. All important, existential matter.

Wherever we end up in a few month's time, these sort of conversations, that are both funny and anxiety provoking to Steven at the same time, will continue. I hear and read all the stuff on best interests and know that nights like last night are what give Steven his quality of life. And long may they continue.

Now, on with the book..........................

I Was a Wartime Code Breaker:

The original idea for the blog was that it would be a mish mash of ideas, experiences and bad jokes. Looking back at the first post though, I can see that I set a theme early on and often return to my favourite subjects (or those that really send my anger into orbit). My debut post ("It's Not What It Says On The Tin") is about the language of the social care world and how much of it is incomprehensible and meaningless. Worse, it often is used to hide another, less favourable agenda.

So, here is a collection of writings about a language that deadens the soul and turns hirsute men bald:

- It's Not What It Says On The Tin
- Let's Talk Money
- Difference – Let's Go Out In The Community

It's Not What It Says On The Tin

April 23, 2012

Language. Language used to create a false reality. Language used to unsettle and wrong foot. That is the subject of today's sermon.

The world of social care has got this art of to a fine T. It uses the language of transparency to slam down the cast iron shutters. In purporting to shed light, it plunges us into darkness.

Many, many times I have been on the receiving end of this cynical manipulation of language to divert attention from the actual truth (usually, with money at the core of the truth). One has to grudgingly admire the aplomb with which the authorities perform this brainwashing. They do it with mirrors. They are empowering me. Their approach to social care is person centred. And when I wake up in the morning feeling thoroughly disempowered do I realise that I've been on the receiving end of the biggest social care centred con trick.

The current fad, the latest illusion is that care plans have at their heart, the person's independence. So, why is that this newly gained independence suddenly feels like I'm trapped; I've lost out big time; my choices evaporate. The greatest independence con trick of recent times occurred in the infamous case of McDonald vs. Kensington & Chelsea. Miss McDonald had managed to live, for some time, reasonably independently in her own home. Due to an unfortunate medical condition, she needed night time assistance to access her commode. Along comes the Royal borough and they decided that to facilitate Miss McDonald's independence, they should stop the night time support and provide the lady with incontinence pads and sheets instead. Not a single acknowledgement of cost savings, K&C acted solely to promote Miss McDonald's independence. I'm sure she is extremely grateful for this new found independence as she lies in her piss night after night. Last December, I was invited to speak at the Legal Action Group Conference, and the over-riding memory of the day was of the many hardened legal professionals still reeling from the cynical manipulation of a needs assessment by Kensington and Chelsea.

I'm embroiled in something similar at the moment, although thankfully it doesn't involve faeces. For the most part of 2010, my 22 year old autistic son was illegally detained by social services in a positive behaviour unit, having gone for three days respite at a local respite facility, familiar to him. Both the respite centre and the positive behaviour unit cause him considerable anxiety and I have to still reassure him daily that the trauma of that experience is in the past. Since he's been back home, respite has come to us and the council pay a support agency top provide a support worker once a fortnight to stay overnight in our home. Now, all of a sudden, Hillingdon council have decided that Steven's independence is at risk with this arrangement. And how will they encourage his independence? By sending him back to the council's respite centre for once a fortnight respite. You see how insidious this is: lets gloss over the fact that he hasn't slept through the night since he got wind of Hillingdon's plan and instead lets applaud that we are developing an independent, albeit traumatised young autistic man.

Let's turn our attention to personalisation and personal budgets; the "where its at" ideology of social care in 2012. Lauded as being the pinnacle of choice and flexibility, many people are bewildered that their reality of personalisation reveals that the limited choice they once had, has now contracted amidst the inflexibility of the RAS system. Under personalisation, each person has a care assessment at which their specific needs are identified. Those care needs are then fed into the RAS (resource allocation system) and converted to a personal budget: a cash figure designed to pay to have those needs met. Proving that transparency is alive and kicking, you try and find out the figures used by your local authority to calculate the personal budget and you'd probably have more luck trying to relaunch a new series of Love Thy Neighbour. The truth is that most local authorities are feeding the RAS with their old direct payment rate, usually about £10 per hour. Now, picture this Debbie Harry. Prior to the flexibility of personalisation, your care plan consisted of 30 support hours a week, which the local authority commissioned a care agency to provide at, say, £15 per hour. A weekly bill of £450. Under personalisation, your needs haven't changed and you still need 30 hours of support per week. The RAS whirls into action and produces a weekly budget of......£300. But hang on a minute mister; prior to personalisation, I was £150 per week better off. The support agency isn't interested in providing the same level of support for £150 a week less. "Ah, but wait, dear service user. Personalisation is all about flexibility. You can commission your own support, tailored exactly to your needs. That's the beauty of choice". The end result of all this choice is that although I have been assessed for needing 30 hours per week support, I can only afford to pay for 20. I've had to reduce my working week by 10 hours and my wages have dropped by £200 per week. The person I care for cannot access some of her weekly activities as she doesn't have the support to go with her. But hey, never mind, I'm feeling excitedly independent.

I know this reads as a cynical, probably bitter piece, but that is where the continual presentation of a false reality leaves you. It's not what it says on the tin. But all is not lost. To retain a stable footing, we have to learn how to decode the language. If I am told repeatedly that they are only acting in my son's best interests, I have to be alert to the possibility that it is someone else's best interests that are in play. If I am presented with the idea that my choices are being widened by the latest flavour of the month, I mustn't be too surprised if it feels like my choices have actually narrowed. If my independence is being trumpeted, be aware that my personal dignity, sense of safety and possibly quality of life, may be compromised. If you're about to have a person centred plan, dont bother reading up on your Carl Rogers but prepare yourself for someone deciding what is best for you.

Someone pointed out to me that people working in the field have it very tough and are under constant pressure. I agree. Perhaps my expectations are too high. But I believe when dealing with the most vulnerable people, the onus to be honest and straight forward is more important than ever. My son is very literal but also, very intuitive and if he is given a message that his instinct tells him is fishy, and then the anxiety cranks up to almost unmanageable levels.

Just imagine how liberated, how independent we will feel if we can decipher the language and be able to stand our ground and retain a sense of our own reality. Now that would be personalisation.

Let's Talk Money

November 1, 2012

Commissioning. Brokerage. Fairer Charging Policy Co-ordination. Resource Allocation Systems. Procurement. Indicative Budgets. This is the financial vocabulary of social care. And it is crucial that any user of social care services gets to grip with it because to be ignorant of the language leaves you languishing in the starting blocks when it comes to arranging care packages.

This isn't meant to be a tutorial in social care economics. I do believe, though, that a course in this very specific modern language would be enormously helpful to all carers embarking on the murky waters and navigating the care system.

No, the message of this post is quite simple – just talk money. It all boils down to that at the end of the day. Every other human, moral, ideological matter comes secondary to the price tag. All the great initiatives either become diluted, or at worst, hijacked by the money agenda. Take personalization and personal budgets – the great liberator for the service user, offering them real choice and flexibility in how they arrange their care. So, you have your FACS assessment (Fairer access to care services) and your needs are identified. Those needs are then fed into a resource allocation system and each need is given a monetary value. These are totted up and out pops your indicative budget – the cash value of your care. Think of it like the Sainsburys' checkout: support with morning bath – £22.50; two to one support in the community – £96.75; support in preparing a meal – £16.26. These figures are made up by the way, because I have no idea what the actual figures are. Apparently, they are called algorithms but very few LAs could answer if you asked them how their algorithms work. (There feels like an old Les Dawson joke in there somewhere).

So, you have your indicative budget, based on …….? and it is more than likely that this budget will bear no relation to the cost of services in your area:

"Excuse me transformation manager – my indicative budget is for £100 but all the care agencies round here charge £200 for the service that I've been identified as needing".

"Ah, but that is the beauty of the personal budget. You have the choice and flexibility to negotiate with the agencies to secure the right service for you".

"But they'll laugh at me transformation manager. I'm offering them half of what they've valued the service at".

"All is not lost. We can go to Panel".

As the excellent Sara Ryan points out in her wonderful blog "My Daft Life", Panel is always referred to mystically. It's not, The Panel, or A Panel but Panel with a capital P. What or who is a Panel? What do they do? How do they do it? You've got more chance discovering some Masonic secrets. One thing we do know is that Panel has the discretion to increase your indicative budget if they determine it doesn't cut the mustard in financially meeting your needs. And you will be excitedly informed that you have been "successful at Panel" as if meeting your basic needs carries a prize. Off to boot camp and then judges' houses.

But as you can see, we are no longer talking about a person or their quality of life; we are talking pounds, shillings and pence. The service user is a financial commodity.

For much of the time, the talk of money is considered unseemly, so you will be directed into talking about more palatable subjects. Like independence. We are not closing down the day centre to save money; we are closing down the day centre to promote your daughter's independence. Now, instead of her making her own lunch at the day centre, we can encourage her independence by wheeling her around the shopping mall where she can stop off for lunch at McDonalds (and by the way, she will have to buy the support worker's filet of fish as well. That will enhance her independence even more). It took me 18 months after the need had been identified to secure a respite package. For much of that time, the discussion focused on Steven's independence and how it would be improved by him taking his respite at the unit where he was illegally detained. I was a fool; I went along with these discussions which included; social stories, subliminal messaging etc etc etc. After a year, the LA agreed to pay a support agency to provide respite at home but they weren't happy about this and insisted it was a temporary arrangement because Steven's independence was being compromised. When that temporary arrangement ended, I did some independent sums. The support agency were charging the LA £168 for overnight support but paying the support worker £55 (gross). I asked him if he would do the work under direct payments for £65 and I submitted a proposal to that effect to the LA. It would lead to the council saving £105. Funnily enough, we stopped talking "independence" and Panel successfully agreed my proposal. You are probably talking about money, even when you think you are talking about something else.

One last thing, and I've mentioned the word twice in this blog, is it's interesting how the word "fairer" has suddenly entered into the social care doublespeak. We have "fairer access to care services" and "fairer charging policies". This is designed to put you on the back foot because the implication is that anything that came before the fairer charging policy was unfair or less fair. But fairer to whom? The service user? The provider? The general council tax payer? As we've seen, the FACS usually produces an indicative budget that won't financially meet the person's needs. is that fairer? If, under the fairer charging policy, I'm having to contribute to the support agency's profits out of my Disability Living Allowance, who is that fairer to? It's a meaningless word. And it's a mean word. It's like being "successful at Panel"; it adds an emotive element to the basic process to disguise the fact it is purely a financial manoeuvre. Nice.

Do your own needs assessment; construct your own care plan; work out your own costing of the package. And talk in those terms and try not to engage in any person centred nonsense.

And so endeth the sermon. As we're talking money – I'll just pass the collection plate around.

Difference: Let's Go Out Into the Community

November 6, 2012

There was a fascinating discussion on Twitter last night about the language applied to the disabled and how so much of a disabled person's life is couched in this strange language. That led me to have a look at the differences between Steven and me:

1. I live in my home. Steven's "current placement is in the family home".

2. When I make a pizza, I'm making a pizza. When Steven makes a pizza, he's "increasing his independence skills", overseen by an OT.

3. If I go to the gym or the pub, I'm going to the gym or the pub. If Steven goes to the gym or the pub, he's out on his community programme.

4. If I hit the table, I'm having a bad day. If Steven hits the table, it is logged and analysed by a psychologist and the positive behaviour team.

5. If I cry, I'm sad about something. If Steve cries, it is logged and analysed by the psychologist and positive behaviour team.

6. If I shout or swear, I'm angry about something. If Steven shouts or swears it is challenging behaviour and new behaviour management plans need to be drawn up.

7. If I select between steak or fish for my tea, I'm making a choice. If Steven selects between steak or fish for tea, he is being empowered.

8. When I was 18, I left school and started work. When Steven was 18, he was transitioned into adult services.

9. I have friends. Steven has a "circle of support and influence".

10. If I go on the train, I'm going on the train. If Steven goes on the train, he's "accessing the community transport".

11. If I'm asked what I want to do with my free time, I'm planning my hobbies. If Steven is asked what he wants to do with his free time, it's his person centred plan.

12. I don't have a transformation manager. Steven has a transformation manager.

13. If I make an unwise choice, I've cocked up. If Steven makes an unwise choice he may be lacking mental capacity.

14. If I sort my CDs into alphabetical order, I'm being a bit anal. If Steven sorts his Mr Bean DVDs into colour order, he is being "inappropriately obsessive".

15. If I eat 2 Mars bars, I'm being a pig. If Steven eats 2 Mars bars he is "challenging boundaries".

16. If I stay at a friend's, I'm staying at a friend's. If Steve stays at a friend's, he is on respite.

17. I take control. Steven is given control.

18. I review my life with a mate in the pub. Steven's life is reviewed at a multi disciplinary meeting.

Please add some of your own………

Decisions, Decisions, Decisions

During the year of the illegal DoLs, I had my first introduction to the Mental Capacity Act. And since that time, whenever a major decision has to be made, Steven has to go through the rigmarole of a mental capacity assessment.

I'd love to be involved in looking into the unfairness of the MCA for a person with disabilities. In order to make a decision about the most fundamental life choices, they have to jump through hoops that would be unheard of for the non learning disabled.

Here are several blogs I've written on the subject:

- Brian Wilson & Capacity
- Mr Bean & The Mental Capacity Assessment
- Straight From The Gut
- Straight From The Gut 2
- Straight From The Gut 3

Brian Wilson & Capacity

September 29, 2012

Even though Steven has been home for nearly two years now, I still get an emotional reaction when he suddenly tells me a story about his life during the year at the positive behaviour unit. The stories that choke me up often have the same theme: Steven trying to communicate something but being ignored.

I've written before how Steven has signature tunes or signature sayings for most people in his life. At the Mencap pool, he always greets Dave with a quick chorus of "Heartbeat". One of the old cab drivers who used to take him to his water aerobics group would be serenaded with "I Will Do Anything For Love But I Won't Do That". I could give many examples of this type of communication.

This afternoon we were having a music session and I played "Sloop John B" by The Beach Boys. It turned out that whenever one of the male workers at the unit was on shift, Steven would greet him with: "I feel so broke up. I want to go home". Steven calls this his "Brian Wilson singing to Keith" (names have been changed to protect the guilty!)

Of course, it had long been decided by the professionals that Steven lacked capacity to decide where he should live but as the IMCA pointed out, that doesn't stop him having and expressing an opinion, or stating his wish. I've read the reports – if this sort of communication was acknowledged at all, which it rarely was, it was dismissed as an example of Steven's "repetitive speech patterns".

I'm pretty sure that the hundreds of logs I received logging Steven hitting out or throwing something, hid this kind of ignored communication. There was never any point in challenging it but I started to assume that at least some of the "incidents" must have followed times when he didn't feel listened to. Needless to say, that sort of valuable information was never recorded in any of the reports.

It's easier to play deaf.

Mr Bean & the Mental Capacity Assessment

October 1, 2012

Today was the day of the mental capacity assessment to determine if Steven has the capacity to manage the money he gets from the damages claim.

It was quite a palaver before we even got to the surgery. Steven's GP is on long-term sick and the other GP who knows him really well is on a month's holiday. It would probably have been very straightforward if either of them had been there. We ended up seeing a very nice GP who had never met Steven before. She wanted to see me first to get some background, so I arranged a ten minute appointment with her and then had to go back home to collect Steven and take him back for a second appointment 20 minutes later.

This is how the conversation went:

GP: Right Steven. Do you agree to your father managing your damages award?

Steven: (long pause) Watching Mr Bean this afternoon.

GP (even longer pause): Good. As I said, are you happy with that?

Steven: (no pause) Steven Neary's happy. Mr Bean's got a kettle stuck on his hand.

Assessment complete.

On a serious note, I often wonder "where does the money go in social care?" Look at the effort that goes into this assessment. Court of Protection instructs a solicitor to arrange the mental capacity assessment. Official solicitor contacts GP to carry out assessment. GP has two appointments to do the assessment and writes her report. The report is returned to the OS to submit the financial deputyship claim to the court. The damages were agreed mid June; it will probably be early 2013 before Steven sees them.

A Mr Bean postscript:

Steven and his two support workers have just returned from the local swimming pool. I'm to expect a phone call from the duty manager as "several" (read one man who doesn't like Steven) people complained about his actions this morning. Steven took his trunks off for 10 seconds when he was in the spa pool. Last Monday's Mr Bean episode was the one where he jumps of the top board and his trunks come off. I asked Steven what happened and he replied "playing Mr Bean". So now we face a ban from his regular Monday trip out and I blame Rowan Atkinson.

Straight From the Gut

December 14, 2012

Lucy Series wrote another wonderful piece yesterday on mental capacity and making decisions. It might seem that I'm forever latching on to her ideas but I do find her writing so inspirational. For the whole post, see here (http://thesmallplaces.blogspot.co.uk/2012/12/thought-provoking-papers-on-capacity.html)

I've had a problem ever since Steven had a mental capacity assessment in 2010, to assess whether he had the capacity to decide where he wanted to live. It was the first time in my life that I've seen decision making under such scrutiny; a professional panel not only judging if somone has the capacity to make a certain decision but insisting the person demonstrate their decision making function. And even then, there was the strongest feeling that the professinal may decide the wrong decision has been made for the wrong reasons. It felt very scary. It seemed very clear to me that Steven was making himself very clear what his opinion was, albeit that it was not the decision the LA wanted him to make. He didn't even need to be asked; he expressed his opinion that he "wanted to live in the Uxbridge house" several times each day and every day. I didn't know until we went to court, how the referral from the LA to the psychiatrist had been made; it turned out both the social worker and her manager wrote to the psychiatrist. This is what Justice Peter Jackson had to say about the referrals in his judgement:

77. "Again on 21 April, the social worker wrote to Steven's psychiatrist, seeking advice. The letter said

> 1. "my overall concern is that Mr Neary wants Steven home. I have spoken to the other professionals involved in Steven's support and the general views are that Steven would be better supported in an environment that could offer him clear boundaries, structured approach, as well as staff that could manage the behaviours that Steven presents." The team manager wrote to the psychiatrist on 26 April in the same vein, saying: "Mr Neary snr is challenging most aspects of what is taking place; it is increasingly likely that this will end up in the Court of Protection as we have major concerns about the idea of Steven returning home to Dad's to live. It is much more likely that we will be looking for a long-term placement for Steven as we feel that this would be in his best

interests." **These letters hardly provided a neutral summary of events as a basis for professional advice. "**

And when we got to the assessment, the psychiatrist phrased the options to Steven in several different ways but on 24 occasions, Steven answered that he wanted to live in the Uxbridge house. He came unstuck once when the doctor asked him: "which is better; the Uxbridge house or M House?" It was the only time Steven didn't answer the Uxbridge house but as I said to the psychiatrist, I think he was confused by the question – to him "better" is what you become after you've been ill. Steven was also challenged to give reasons why he liked the Uxbridge house and he came up with five reasons: like to live with Dad; like to watch my DVDs; like to listen to my CDs; like to play on my computer; like to see my friends. He only came up with one reason for M House (watching TV – which is the only answer he could have given because that is all he did there). So, by the end of the 2 hour assessment, I believed that not only had Steven been very clear in making a decision; he had also been able to demonstrate that he could explain the reasons behind his preference. He failed the assessment.

It appears to me that the emphasis in a mental capacity assessment is always on a cognitive decision-making process; a feeling based decision or a gut based decision is not considered worthy of capacity. And that's my big problem because that is a ludicrous way of expecting any human being to make a decision.

I work as a counsellor, and typically in that field the two stock, cliché questions from counsellor to client are: "how do you feel about that?" or "what do you think about that?" The more I do this work; I know that the question that I ask the most is: "what does your gut have to say about that?" The head, the heart and the gut – we have to use all three and listen to all three when making a major life decision. Obviously we have to engage the head and look at the pros and cons of the options open to us. But our head can't be the only organ used because it edits stuff. Likewise, it's important to engage the heart and consider how we feel about the choices but we can get overwhelmed by our feelings and sometimes can't see the wood for the trees. For me, the gut is the most reliable of the organs we use in our decision-making process – it's where our truth lies. We may not always hear the answer we want but we will receive the truth. It gets tricky though because sometimes it's very hard to communicate to others what we have heard from our gut, as the gut has a language all of its own. And if I'm in a mental capacity assessment, I know that I've got to do my best to express myself and let's face it, professionals tend to be at their most comfortable with a cognitive argument.

Every day for the past 14 years I have sat in a counselling room with people wrestling with huge life changing decisions; do I leave my wife; do I change my career; do I move to be nearer the family; do I give up drugs; do I want to confront the person who sexually abused me; do I try to get to grips with my obsessive compulsive disorder (The list is endless)? I don't have any formal research statistics to support this statement but the vast majority of people I have seen, end up following their gut decision, wherever that decision may lead them. I have been seeing a woman who has been trying to decide whether to resolve a nasty work situation by going to an industrial tribunal. We've spent weeks weighing up the pros and cons of that option, and she often ends up thinking that she probably wouldn't be successful. We've examined how she feels about the choice and then her feelings of rage, sadness and impotency overpower her. The other day, I asked her to see if her gut had a take on all of this. She immediately looked startled. She smiled and said the response she got was: "Go for it. It's going to be bloody hard and you may get bruised but you may come out of it a much stronger, wiser person". And that is what she is going to do. I wonder how that would stand up at a mental capacity assessment.

One other thought – we are also allowed not to make a choice too. And we're allowed to go for any easy option because we don't want the hassle of the harder one. Or perhaps we are too fearful to make a decision. That is okay too.

But a disabled person, undergoing a mental capacity assessment isn't allowed these human traits of uncertainty, decisions based on fear, and most importantly, decisions from the gut. I could choose tomorrow, to leave everything I know and go and travel the world in a camper van. It could be a terrible decision but i can do it. A disabled person wouldn't be allowed to make that decision. That can't be right.

Straight From the Gut 2

December 19, 2012

Following last week's blog post on determining mental capacity (and the blog by Lucy Series that inspired it), I have been blown away by the messages I've received and the conversations that have followed from it. There appears to be a very real interest in incorporating gut/intuitive responses into mental capacity assessments alongside the more measurable, cognitive responses. The general view is that this has to become part of the MCA so that it levels the playing field for the learning disabled. In fact, as one professional from the field commented, it has to happen because as things stand at the moment, to solely rely on cognitive decision-making functioning is discriminatory. The non learning disabled can draw on many processes when making decisions; why can't the learning disabled?

The very nature of a mental capacity assessment and the fact that they tend to be applied to the very big life decisions puts an enormous unfair burden on the person being assessed. The MCA requires a person to be able to express and explain their cognitive process about the important decision to a collection of professionals, who may have already judged what they believe the "right" decision to be.

Just imagine that you were required to consult, be assessed and get agreement from a body of professionals if you had to make any of the following decisions:

- Where you want to live.
- How you spend your money.
- Whether, and where you go on holiday.
- Whether you can marry the partner of your choice.
- Whether you can have sex with the partner of your choice.

Even if the non learning disabled were prepared to put themselves through this rigorous scrutiny, think how night impossible it would be if you had to produce a cognitive, reasoned balance sheet for all of these decisions. You can't bring intuition into it; you can't bring feelings into it – your reasoning parameters are extremely narrow. But this is the requirement for the learning disabled, albeit borne out of an incentive to protect them.

I am advocating that assessment encompasses other processes by which people make decisions; namely their gut intuition and their feelings. Not only should the assessment include these processes but that they should carry as equal a weight as the more measurable, cognitive processes.

Perhaps the big problem is the fundamental perception of an "assessment". An assessor asks a question and the assessed is expected to supply an answer. This happens usually in the stark setting of a psychiatrist's office. That may be a tiny bit restrictive! by all means, ask questions but be prepared to accept that some of the responses may be hard to articulate from a reasoned position. Because the answers come from the gut or the heart and not from the head.

I would suggest that it's futile to try to determine something as important as mental capacity in a formal 90 minute interview. It requires much more time in both formal and informal environments; carefully recording the person's verbal, physical, emotional, intuitive, behavioural reactions. If a learning disabled person doesn't understand or respond to your question, possibly, just possibly, the problem may be in the way you've asked the question.

We need a new model in assessing mental capacity. Anyone interested?

Postscript:

Here is a conversation I heard on the bus this afternoon between Betty and May:

Betty: "I still can't decide if we're having turkey or pork".

May: "You're cutting it a bit fine".

Betty: "I like the taste of pork but I'm not too keen on the smell",

May: "Have turkey then".

Betty: "Bob's gone off it. Do you remember that year he was queer on it?"

May: "We're having a duck".

Betty: "DUCK?"

(Long pause)

Betty: "What you having duck for?"

May: "My mother loved a nice duck".

Betty: "Ah. There you go then".

An analysis of their decision reasoning:

No to pork – unpleasant smell.

Not to turkey – turned Bob queer.

Yes to duck – mother loved it.

Straight From the Gut 3

February 11, 2013

I know. I know. I'm becoming a bit obsessive about the hoops a learning disabled person has to go through to demonstrate their decision making capacity but I heard two stories on Saturday that show how the majority of us make our decisions.

Firstly, someone was telling me about choosing a pre-school nursery for his daughter. They visited five in their area and read the Ofsted reports on all of them. One of his most telling statements was: "we sat down after visiting the five nurseries and tried to match what we had seen to their Ofsted reports. They didn't match at all". In the end, they made their decision by talking to other parents they knew locally and relying on their instinctive reactions to the places.

Later, I spoke to a man who had been looking at care homes for his mother who has dementia. He had visited three and like the other chap, had read the CQC inspection reports on all of them. Alarmingly, he told me about the one that had the most glowing report – he was shown one of the bedrooms and saw blood stains over the bare mattress. As he said; "It may have been fine but I don't want to send my mother off to the Blair Witch Project". The second one he visited, he declined on the basis that 18 people were sitting in a lounge, doing nothing and only two staff were attending to them. In the end, he made his choice because the staff smiled warmly at him and the residents looked to be doing something.

I wonder how these two decisions would have stood up under the scrutiny of a mental capacity assessment.

From Action Man Dolls to Grown Up DoLs

The judgement in Neary Vs Hillingdon opened up a wide debate about the Deprivation of Liberty safeguards. Reading other judgements since, it has felt to me like one step forwards, two steps back. We await the outcome of the Cheshire appeal, as at the moment, nobody really knows where they stand with the current legislation.

I've been lucky over the past year to have attended conferences and met best interest assessors who are nothing like the ones I encountered at Hillingdon. The amount of training BIAs get varies alarmingly across the country. The worst (guess where?) is ½ day on the MCA, HRA and the DoLs legislation.

And whilst the legal people, the social care professionals and the politicians discuss the Act, there are real people at the mercy of it who, not to put too fine a point on it, are fucked.

- The Vacuum Of The DoLs
- No DoL – No Chance

The Vacuum of The DoLs

July 17, 2012

Today saw the publication from the NHS Information Centre of their third annual DoLs report for 2011/12. (The full report is here: http://www.ic.nhs.uk/webfiles/publications/005_Mental_Health/dols2011-12/mca_dols_eng_2011_12_3rd_rep.pdf)

There's an awful lot of figures and statistics in this report: I needed a Red Bull to help me get through it. This blog is just a series of thoughts and questions that popped up for me whilst trying to absorb it.

The first big stat is that during 2011/12, 56% of all DoLs were authorised; meaning of course that 44% weren't authorised. So, here are my first two questions:

1. How many of the 56% of DoLs authorisations were challenged? I think it would be rash to assume that all of the 56% were necessary, appropriate, or indeed lawful.

2. What happened to the 44% that weren't authorised? Presumably these people were in a care home or hospital – are they still there but not under a DoL?

The number of authorisations has increased steadily since the safeguards were introduced in 2010. However, for the most recent quarter (December 2011 to March 2012), the figures went down for the first time. Is it a coincidence that this drop coincides with the Cheshire ruling (Thank goodness, that is going to appeal). DoLs are only meant to be authorised for up to a year, so what have happened to all those people whose DoL has passed a year? No explanation for the drop is given in the report, which I find quite worrying.

As in previous reports, there is an enormous variation in the number of DoLs sought across the country. The latest report reveals a variance from 0 to 463. I find it very hard to believe that the LAs who declared 0 authorisations, don't have anyone in their care homes or hospitals who are being deprived of their liberty? Without external scrutiny, it must be quite possible for people to be left in a home or hospital with no safeguards being applied. There are at least two members of the Get Steven Home group who have relatives in a care home and both the person and their family don't want them to be in the home but have found it impossible to persuade the LA to authorise a DoL. And without a DoL, a challenge becomes very difficult.

Following on from that, there isn't a single mention in the report of IMCAs. There are enough judgements out there now stressing the entitlement to an IMCA but they obviously weren't considered important enough to make it into the report. So, my question is how many of the 56% of authorisations were referred to the IMCA service?

I had an horrendous experience with the Hillingdon Best Interest Assessors but having attended the Yorkshire DoLs conference and having met several committed assessors on-line, I know that my experience wasn't typical. One of my favourite stats is that 93 DoLs authorisations were not granted by the supervisory body but the BIA insisted that a deprivation of liberty was occurring. That shows that 93 people were prepared to challenge the supervisory body. The report does flag up the potential conflict if interest for BIAs when they are employed by the supervisory body. I don't believe the BIAs in our case were incompetent; I believe they were weak and allowed themselves to be told what to write by their managers. Hopefully, they are in the minority.

I know it wasn't the remit of the report but I would love to know some of the stories behind the statistics. How else does one make sense of the 44% of cases where a DoL wasn't authorised? What does that mean for the lives of those people? Have their lives improved or got back on track as a result of not being under a DoL? Someone wrote to me the other week about her son who has been in a "temporary" care home for four years; he went there for an assessment. Last summer after several DoLs cases hit the news, his parents asked the home to consider a DoL. They met with the BIA for four hours and he agreed that a DoL was occurring. However, his report was squashed and a DoL wasn't authorised. The young man is still in the home without a DoL.

Overall, the report leaves me wanting more. I'd love someone to take the DoLs by the scruff of the neck and review them from beginning to end. The NHS report relies on the returns from LAs and NHS trusts. This is only one part of the story. What about the monitoring of the initial stage of the process – does anyone look into the fact that some LAs aren't authorising a single DoL. Why? Where are their residents safeguards? And what about the data from the courts? Are LAs/NHS trusts referring all matters of dispute to the courts? How many people have been released from their detainment by the courts? These seem to me important figures to understand how the Act is working?

This report feels like it exists in a vacuum. I feel like I've read one part of a trilogy but the other parts aren't available to me.

No DoL – No Chance?

July 31, 2012

This is a complete work of fiction.

A friend of mine has been in court recently in an attempt to challenge her Local Authority's decision that it is in her relatives' best interests to live in a care home. The court has declared that none of the parties, the local authority or the care home can be disclosed, so my apologies that this post may read a little vague at times.

The judge decided that he was going along with the LA's decision, although he raised the question whether the same decision would have been arrived at, if the case had come before the court sooner. He decided that after two years in the care home, the relative would be "settled" and a move, either back to her home or to alternative accommodation would not be in her best interests. I understand a certain logic in that but my unease comes from how the outcome could have been very different for the lady if the Local Authority had carried out the proper process at the time.

A couple of years back, when she was in her early nineties, the lady had a fall at her home. She was admitted to hospital but lack of beds meant she was quickly discharged to a care home. She has been there ever since, although nobody at the time agreed that this would be a long-term arrangement. Both the lady and her family assumed that at some point, she would return to her home. After a few months, my friend started to ask questions; normal questions that a concerned relative might ask – most notably, what were the plans for her relative returning home? This is interesting in itself – already the power balance had shifted – my friend was asking others what their decision was. She was quite clear that she wanted her grandmother to come home; the relative wanted to return home but something told her that it wasn't her decision to make. This is such a common trap that we carers fall into.

So, we have a person in a care home asking to go home and her family asking for her to go home. Surely we are now in Deprivation of Liberty territory. Only, in this case one was never authorised. The lady has remained in the home for two years without a Deprivation of Liberty authorisation (DoL). The consequences of this have been very costly and I don't just mean financial):

My friend had to take the lead in trying to bring the case to court. This took two years from the time her relative was first admitted to the home. Trying to find legal representation was near impossible. But if a DoL had been served, the relative could have been represented by the official solicitor and assuming my friend would have been appointed her RPR, she would have been entitled to legal aid as well. None of that happened and now my friend faces huge costs. Also, if a DoL had been authorised, then the case would have come to court much sooner and the whole business of the lady being "settled" might have been seen very differently. A DoL would have to had included the lady and her family's objection to the placement and a decent stab at a best interests assessment would have had to have taken place, addressing the point which the LA seemed determined to avoid – was there a lesser restrictive option for her care available? Once again, this didn't happen. It seems to me there were several breaches to the lady's human rights going on here.

My friend, after two years of fighting, is exhausted and is letting the matter rest. I know that feeling; I am still experiencing health issues that I am convinced are the result of my two-year long battle. My friend was in a very similar situation to me; the LA withheld important information from her and she was excluded from much of the process. To have to fight every single step of the way, when you are being blindfolded most of the time is an exhausting exercise.

There has been a lot of discussion recently about the latest DoLs figures issued by the Department of Health. At the time I felt there was something really important missing – how many people are there in care homes or hospitals without a DoL, where it is clear there should be a standard authorisation in place. We will never know the answer to that as the machinery isn't there to monitor when this is happening. I know from letters that I get that there are many people completely trapped because they know enough from the Neary vs Hillingdon case that a DoL should be in place but they can't get the managing authority to serve one.

Justice Peter Jackson said that authorities must not use DoLs as a means of getting their own way – does this story show that some authorities may **not** be using DoLs as a means of getting their way?

This completely imaginary case shows that there could be a lot of it about.

The Professional Input

In his report for the court, the expert psychologist witness made several recommendations for Steven's support package. Amongst those, was the value of the input of a whole team of professionals: psychologist; speech and language therapist; occupational therapy. Hillingdon duly sprung into life and provided such a team and for the first 18 months at home, I would meet with the team at least once a month.

I hope this collection of posts doesn't read that I'm intolerant of any external input; I'm intolerant of bad external input. Many times I've cried out for someone to take a look at our situation and suggest ways in which our lives could be better. Unfortunately, as a result of not taking the time to get to know Steven, most of the input turned out to be a hindrance rather than a help:

- We Wish You a Person Centred Christmas
- Taken With a Pinch Of SALT
- There'll Be Some Sweet Sounds From The Nightshift
- The Stench of Bad Psychology
- Who Let The Logs Out
- Playing Games With The Vulnerable
- None The Wiser
- Sudden Endings

We Wish You A Person Centred Christmas

December 5, 2012

'Tis the season to be jolly, so just for once, I thought I'd write a blog brimming with Yuletide cheer. The decorations are up and the tree is dressed here at our current residential placement. On the big day, we will be toasting our independence and celebrating the choice and flexibility in our lives by choosing between a tub of Cheeselets and a tub of cheese footballs (or "cheesy bollocks" as Steven calls them, in tribute to Neil Morrissey from Men Behaving Badly). Daringly, in the finest person centred tradition, we may even opt to eat both tubs. And to hell with the Pringles.

I've self assessed our Christmas needs; turkey, trifle, Mr Bean DVD and fed them into the resource allocation system. And guess what? Out popped a tin of spam, a tapioca pudding and a cine film of Benny Hill on the beach at Frinton on Sea. Unfortunately, Panel are out on their Christmas Do, but if the spam doesn't completely meet our needs, I can always enter into negotiations with an alternative service provider for an equitable chunk of luncheon meat.

Before the big day arrives, we anticipate the visit of three wise men bearing their own seasonal gifts. The transformation manager will arrive with a gift wrapped indicative budget, empowering us to creatively cut back on the support we receive next year. The housing manager will descend angelically with an eviction notice, but don't worry; I've got my eye on a well-appointed supported living stable. And bringing up the rear will be the Personalisation Champion with a lovely Christmassy bill from the fairer charging policy team, wishing us a prosperous 2013. It will be a delightful gathering and too much to hope that they'll stay and join in with our "Stop the Cavalry" karaoke.

Amidst the cards we receive from our family, friends and circle of support will be a glorious parcel from our cuddly in-house psychologist; a selection of festive logs. Behaviour logs. Diet Logs. Incident Report logs. Goodness me, we'll be well replenished with all those logs.

Christmas wouldn't be Christmas without a nice board game. No Cluedo or Operation for us at the community living unit. We've got a personalised occupational therapy game – "How to Unwrap a Present in 24 Monitored Stages". It's absorbing. You score the service user on a scale from 0 to 5 taking factors into account like: concentration capacity; degree of independence shown; understanding of task. Imagine my glee if I can score Steven a resounding "5" as he unwraps his Gipsy Kings' CD (Don't ask – he's been requesting it for months). It's a shame that Christmas Day is for one day only because I won't get the chance to test him on the advanced level – ribbons!

Sadly, my carer's assessment hasn't delivered anything festive; in fact it hasn't delivered anything at all. But bon voyage to all at the staff at the carers centre as they sail off for a well-earned Christmas break on the Algarve. Compared to the funds of the carers grant, Steven's £10 DLA Christmas bonus may seem small change but it will pay for him to top up his tan for ten minutes at the Virgin Active. And like a shepherd, I will watch over my flock on Christmas night, as I do every other night, as the respite allocation manager has gone on a fact finding respite trip to Lapland to find out how the Laplanders allocate their respite. He'll report back in April, apparently.

I'll be rushed off my feet with all the preparations. I've risk assessed the living room for tinsel hazards; I've got a behaviour management plan on standby in case the new Coldplay DVD induces a meltdown. And if it should snow, we might access the community and go out on our balcony and lob a snowball at a jolly neighbour in the spirit of positive social interaction. Remember kids – inclusion is for life, not just at Christmas.

It's going to be a great day though. The support workers have the day off, so it'll just be me and Steven. We'll eat what we want, watch as much Abba and Fawlty Towers as we want and sing our hearts out to the Gipsy Kings. Just for one day out of 365, we will experience a truly person centred day. Join me in an advocaat.

Taken With A Pinch of SALT

June 18, 2012

This morning I had a meeting with Steven's sixth speech and language therapist (commonly known as a SALT) in two years. The purpose of the meeting was to introduce a new social story to Steven. Since my last spell of illness in 2009 that led to Steven being kept away from his home for a year, he understandably has an ongoing anxiety about me becoming sick again. I regularly have to deal with the anxious enquiry if ever I cough or sneeze: "Dad's not getting that flu again?" The idea of this latest social story is to help Steven manage his anxiety around illness.

Help, No seriously, please help. I have no idea, despite years of practice, of how to deal with absurdities like this. I feel like I've taken a serum of nonsense and become paralysed as a result.

The SALT laid the terms of this project by reassuring me that it was a collaborative process and how important it was that I and the support workers take the lead in introducing the story to Steven and monitoring its impact. She then presented me with the story she'd already written; a list of instructions in how to deliver it and a reporting log to record Steven's reaction to the story and measure outcomes. There was also a subtext during this induction. The SALT had observed two of Steven's support workers working with him whilst he was making his Friday pizza and she was concerned that they "related to him in different ways". I know what I'm meant to say at this point but instead I said that I think it is fabulous that Steven, a man with severe autism, is able to build completely unique, individual relationships with each of his support workers and I'm proud that he can relate to them as individuals. That was the wrong answer.

The social story is called: "When Someone Is Ill" and consists of the following five pages:

Page one: "When someone is ill their body can feel many different things".

Page two: "Their body might hurt. This can include one or more of the following: headache, sore throat, chest hurts, stomach ache, backache".

Page three: "They might have a snottty nose or they might have a cough".

Page four: "When someone starts to feel ill there are many ways to help them feel better. They might need to: get some rest, see a doctor, take some medicine".

Page five: "These things are for helping them to feel better so they can go back to finishing their work and doing fun activities".

Accepting the invitation that "your feedback is welcome Mr Neary", I tentatively suggested that Steven would struggle with the length of the sentences and several of the words contained therein. It is not the language he uses and the vague terms are ones he finds very hard to follow. That was the wrong feedback. Meeting arranged for a weeks' time to review how the introduction has gone.

We end the meeting with the SALT informing me that there is "no right or wrong way in how Steven reacts to the story", alerting me immediately that there is a right and wrong way in her eyes. I didn't want to burden the support workers with the first read through, but remembering that one of the instructions is to only read the story when Steven is in a receptive and settled mood, I spot a window of opportunity for later. Steven's morning support worker clocks off at 2.30 and the other worker who will be covering for my respite night will be clocking on at 5pm. Steven has already planned that he and I watch the Fawlty Towers episode "Gourmet Night" ("Ducks off") which he finds hysterical. I decide to read the story between Basil and Countdown starting. I read the story verbatim and when we've got to page two, Steven said "Put it away Dad". My instinct tells me that this will be seen as a wrong reaction and if I stop reading my reaction will be wrong too, so I persist. By the time I get to the end, Steven has said "put it away Dad" four times and by the time Countdown starts, his mood is much less settled. Where is his empathy: doesn't he realise I've got a monitoring form to complete and describing what has happened is likely to be problematic come next week's meeting.

Here are a few random thoughts I've had since Jonathon solved today's Countdown conundrum:

1) Is it okay to change the content and language of the story?

2) Will the outcome be another tick in the box of Mr Neary being an uncooperative parent?

3) Why, as Hillingdon close all their day centres, is it okay for so much energy to be given to stuff like this?

4) How much does the SALT earn and could that money go towards the closing day centres?

5) Does anybody understand autism?

6) Does anybody understand Steven?

7) If I pretend next week that everything went well, will I be marked down as "disguised compliance"?

8) Why, whenever I go to these meetings, does there feel like so many elephants in the room, I want to sing the Marching Song from The Jungle Book?

9) We have been under social care for the past 8 years. Why, as each year passes, does it feel that the gulf between what could be useful and what is actually delivered, seem bigger?

As I said earlier, please help. This sort of situation disturbs me and I know that my head will be full to bursting between now and next week's meeting on how to present this at the meeting. And it doesn't matter at all that my gut tells me that I should be giving this no energy whatsoever. Why does person centred support feel so stressful and disempowering?

There'll Be Some Sweet Sounds, Coming Down, From The Night Shift

June 19, 2012

Thank you so much everyone for your messages and posts after yesterday's blog post about the SALT and the social story.

I woke up this morning and it was quite clear. The problem with the story was not just the language and the vague content but more importantly, that the context of the story was all wrong. Steven doesn't get worried about my health out of empathy for me; he worries about what it means for him. And after the experience of 2009, he always worries that he is going to be taken away. The health thing is a red herring – if ever I'm away, it prompts anxiety in him.

So, I've completely re-written the social story and the focus is on "Night Shift". Why do we have a support worker stay over to do a night shift; who does it, and what happens to Steven when a night shift happens. As our whole live is a musical, we end the story with a quick burst of the Commodores (I know it doesn't quite scan but if we sing fast, it'll work).

This is it:

Night Shift

What Is Night Shift?

Night shift is when our friends sleep downstairs in the Uxbridge house

Steven Neary sleeps upstairs in his bedroom in the Uxbridge house

Who Does Night Shift?

- § **Michael does night shift at the Uxbridge house**

- § **Alan does night shift at the Uxbridge house**

- § **Ishmael does night shift at the Uxbridge house**

We Have Night Shift When ……

- § **Dad goes to his meeting with Ian**

- § Dad is sleeping at counselling work
- § Dad has a nasty cold
- § Our friend's bed is broken
-

Where Is Steven Neary?

When our friends do night shift, Steven Neary sleeps in his bedroom upstairs in the Uxbridge house.

Steven Neary sleeps in the Uxbridge house every day.

Night Shift by The Commodores

"And if Dad's not at home

Steven's not on his own

Ishmael's on the nightshift"

The Stench of Bad Psychology

June 27, 2012

How do you get rid of a destructive, manipulative psychologist? No, it's not the opening line of a joke. It's a question I've been wrestling with for over a year.

In February 2011, the psychologist expert appointed by the Court of Protection to report on Steven and his best interests wrote an excellent report. It was instrumental in the judge's decision that Steven could live in his own home permanently. In his report, he identified some areas that he believed would benefit Steven, input from external professionals, like occupational therapy, speech therapy and, psychology. Absolutely fine and welcome. Unfortunately, the matter was left with Hillingdon to arrange the input and where they have an in-house service, they will not look for a more appropriate resource elsewhere. You may remember the year long battle I have had to arrange respite. Hillingdon assessed a need for respite but the only option they would fund was the very unit where Steven was detained for a whole year against his Article 5 & 8 Human Rights. Thankfully that is all sorted but there has been a more insidious, troublesome issue rumbling away.

An in-house psychologist was appointed to Steven's care team in the autumn of 2010. Steven was still in the positive behaviour unit at the time and the council were well into their plan of moving him to the hospital in Wales. It was never clear what her role was at the time; lots of talk about "coordinating processes" and "facilitating dialogues". One of the dialogues she had with one of the workers at the unit, who fortunately hadn't left their integrity at the door when they clocked on was that "Mr Neary is the tough nut we have to crack". And I was duly called to meet her for the first time. I think I would have preferred to have had four wisdom teeth extracted with a spoon. It was a deeply dispiriting experience and she wouldn't let me leave the room until I came up with five positive things about Steven's experience in the positive behaviour unit. Fortunately, I put my SAS training to good use and scaled the Civic centre walls and made my escape.

Fast forward six months and Steven was now at home and a team was assembled to deliver his care. All agreed that this psychologist would have a valuable role in coordinating all the support and her input on Steven's behaviour would be important.

One area where she has had considerable input has been in form design. We now have a log for daily purposes. This log has to include; what Steven has ate, what activities he has done, what independent tasks he has carried out, what his mood and behaviour has been like; how have the support staff and myself dealt with any difficult behaviours. I now have over 500 of these sheets. 500 statements like "Had pears, bananas, grapes, satsuma's for breakfast", "Put his pyjamas in the washing machine", "Watched Countdown calmly". And every month the team pour over these sheets suggesting how the forms could be amended to produce more useful data.

On top of the daily log, we have an "incident log" and an "incident log summary". The incident log is an A4 document that is intended to describe any incidents of challenging behaviour that occur. This form has been through many versions. The summary is a table for each month that looks like this:

Date	Incident	Near Miss	Description
1.5.12	0	0	
2.5.12	0	0	
3.5.12	0	1	Steven attempted to throw book at Dad
4.5.12	0	0	
5.5.12	0	0	

And so on and so forth….. Our friend is then meant to analyse the documents and offer her professional support in changing or managing whatever she identifies as amiss.

This might be a productive exercise if she didn't have such an obvious hidden agenda. Sadly, she is still trying to crack that tough nut. She is a corporate tool, still in a litigatious place, where the function is to find fault at anyone involved in Steven's care (outside of the council's own staff). All the dialogue seems geared to one thing – a return to court and Hillingdon being able to say "We told you so". Never mind that this tactic failed horribly for them a year ago and the judge berated them for trying to find evidence to support a theory they had invented and after a year in their care, they had been unable to build any evidence that was truthful.

Here's a flavour of what I mean. I sometimes forget to send the logs off. Remiss of me I know but sometimes I might prefer to be watching a DVD or having a music session with Steven. In March, I was a month behind, so submitted two months worth of logs. I was shocked to find that the psychologist had arranged an urgent meeting on receipt of the logs to:" review how incidents are being recorded and managed, given the recent escalation in aggressive behaviours and review how anxiety is being recorded and managed". And what was this "recent escalation in aggressive behaviours"? Well, in February we had three incidents; in March we had four! Fuck – batten down the hatches, things are escalating out of control. (For those statisticians reading this, in April we had two incidents by the way).

A week later, the psychologist suddenly turned up at my meeting with Steven's dietician. Do psychologists do that?

A few days later, she requested dates and times of all Steven's community activities, so she could "observe" the support staff dealing with him. There was no way I could put Steven's hard working team in that position because the agenda is so murky.

And to the latest encounter that has prompted this piece. Yesterday was the latest two monthly meeting. "Incidents" have remained at 2/3 per month. It would be great if it was 0 but we are dealing with someone with autism here and the awful meltdowns that accompany the condition. Unfortunately one of the recent incidents happened in the day centre Steven attends each Friday and was witnessed by the new speech therapist. So, off we're launched again. Redesign of forms for clearer data; training for all the staff; observations etc etc etc. The support worker had completed the daily log form and one of the day centre's own incident reports but had forgotten to do our own incident report. Bring back hanging eh? In the midst of all the earnest discussion, the psychologist said "and of course, we don't want another airport incident". It was low, and mean, and possibly unethical. The judge pulled them up on it last year; firstly for the lack of supervision during the incident and secondly in how Hillingdon tried to use the incident to smear Steven in that appalling press release they circulated. And one year one, they are still doing it. I pointed out to her that not only was she dismissing the work done by myself, the support staff and Steven himself but also her own colleagues who have worked hard in the five years since the airport incident. She just smiled.

I have made two complaints now and said that I will not be engaging with her but each meeting she bounces back like an aggressive Tigger. I've thought about reporting her to her professional body; as a counsellor myself, I am aware of the ethical standards that exists within the various bodies and I'm sure she must be breaking several of hers.

It is sickening that after being crucified by a High Court judge, being pilloried in the press and as I found out last week at the DoLs conference, being used nationally as the worst example of bad practice, nothing fundamentally changes in the attitude.

And as usual, we're left with not having a service that could actually be quite useful to Steven.

Who Let The Logs Out

July 9, 2012

I've made a decision. It's a decision that will probably get me into trouble but I'm in a "what the fuck" mood.

I've written before that my life consists of recording every single aspect of Steven's life for the professionals involved in his care package to scrutinise. Here is the current list of logs we have to keep:

1) Diet Log: Every single piece of food or drink that Steven consumes is recorded for the dietician.

2) START Incident Form: This is a very thorough document that goes into fine detail of any incident (or "near miss") of Steven doing something untoward. This form goes to the psychologist and the positive behaviour team.

3) Daily Activities: This lists everything that Steven does during the day from having a bath; going to the gym; watching Daybreak etc.

4) Independence Logs: This is for the occupational therapist and covers anything that Steven does for himself and includes: applying deodorant; putting his clothes into the washing machine; packing his swimming gear into his bag.

5) Mood & Behaviour Logs: Another one for the psychologist – every mood change is carefully recorded and reasons why he might go from content to anxious considered.

6) Social Story Monitoring Chart: This is for the speech therapist and traces Steven's reaction to the "Night Shift" story by recording his reaction at four stages during the course of the narrative.

7) Monthly Log Summary: Everyone gets a copy of this. It's a monthly summary of any incidents of challenging behaviour.

I'm sure you'll agree that's an awful lot of recording. We don't live in a house – we live in an observation chamber. It's a life under a microscope. It's a good job that Steven doesn't understand irony because one of his favourite music videos is the Simply Red version of The Air That I Breathe (http://www.youtube.com/watch?v=hfbAKZTM3-A). That's what our life feels like most of the time.

As I write this, Steven has been back at home for 542 days, which means that we have completed 542 daily logs. 542 times someone has written that Steven made his bed or had a glass of milk at 5pm. For the first four months, I religiously scanned these documents and sent them off to the professionals for their observations. And for the first four months, I didn't get a single response, except for the suggestion that the forms be extended to include even more data. So, I stopped sending the daily reports and now, once a month, the support worker's manager collects them and files them away somewhere.

I really like Steven's dietician; she's a warm-hearted, down to earth woman. She did initially analyse the daily diet logs and recommended nine changes to Steven's daily intake. Not rocket science; just good sensible advice. I implemented all the suggestions and more, but unfortunately Steven's weight gain has accelerated since the diet began. And that is the end of that input, although, I'm still asked to record everything he eats or drinks.

My guess is that the council use students on placement for their SALT and OT posts. We haven't had an occupational therapist since before Christmas but up to that point, their emphasis had been almost compulsively focused on encouraging Steven's independence. The big project of 2011 was pizza making and I got through a whole pack of printer paper recording the progress of that activity. The process of making a pizza was broken down to 28 stages and each stage had to be marked on a scale from 0-5, depending on Steven's skill and commitment to the task. Since December, my independence logs probably disappear into a person centred void.

As I described in my previous blog post, my big problem is with the psychologist, who is clearly still in litigation mode rather than support mode. We meet every two months where she is ever critical of the lack of information contained in the START incident forms and instead puts her spin on our life with phrases like: "an escalation in aggressive behaviours". She doesn't mention the monthly summaries where the figures last month shot through the roof from 2 incidents in May to 3 incidents in June! She has been on our case since Summer 2010 and I don't think I'm being unfair when I say that I cannot recall one single positive contribution she's made in two years. But the recording forms are probably three times as long as they were two years ago.

Anyway, I'm ranting. What is my big decision?

Last week, we spent five days in Great Yarmouth. I did all the packing on Sunday night and when our support worker arrived on Monday, he put the big blue binder containing all the forms/logs into the suitcase. I took it straight out again. I wanted to experience five days out from under the microscope. And it was wonderful. One meltdown when I went to get the keys to the caravan and waited in a queue for 80 minutes and a mini meltdown when Steven realised that they didn't have a ghost train at Pleasurewood Hills. Both meltdowns were contained and lasted about 20 minutes each; that's 40 minutes out of the 7200 minutes we were away.

I'm not doing any more logs.

I will use the big blue binder to file the utility bills instead,

If someone asks me what Steven had for breakfast, I will rely on my memory rather than a log.

You can see from this narrative that the piles and piles of paperwork are not about analysis or professional intervention. It is simply recording for recording sake. When we were in court, Hillingdon made a big thing about me "under reporting incidents". That was their only explanation for the enormous increase in incidents whilst Steven was in the positive behaviour unit. I was able to truthfully say that I had never once been asked for the logs in the 18 months that they had instructed me to keep them. Nobody had been interested.

Perhaps I expect too much. Perhaps I am wrong to assume that the exercise has any other purpose than recording an autistic man's life. Perhaps I've mis-interpreted something as the king's new clothes. And perhaps cosmetic intervention is the best that can be offered.

One thing that I'm sure of is that if I had been working with one of my clients for two years and they couldn't think of one valuable intervention I'd made, I'd be deeply ashamed.

Like Mick Hucknall broke free from his observation bubble at the end of the Simply Red video, so I want to release myself from a life of claustrophobic scrutiny. It would be really nice for Steven and I to watch an episode of Mr Bean without the event being recorded on a log. It would be even nicer for Steven to have a meltdown and not feel that recording it will be used against him in the future.

So, apart from a chocolate Yuletide one, the Uxbridge house will now be a log free zone.

CRAZY POSTSCRIPT:

I wrote this blog during a gap at work this morning. I've had the idea of stopping the logs since we were away last Thursday but haven't mentioned it to anyone.

I got home today just after 1pm and Steven was out with his support workers. Because it usually holds such a prominent place on the dining room table, I immediately noticed that the massive blue binder was missing.

This is what happened. Probably at exactly the same time that I was writing this blog, Steven was getting very agitated about me going out this evening and threw the folder out of the living room window. We live in a first floor flat, so it landed in the hedge below. There was just the one support worker on duty at the time, so he couldn't go out and retrieve it and by the time the second support worker arrived, the whole thing had gone missing from the hedge. A few pages of daily logs were stuck in the leaves but everything else was gone. No risk assessments. No incident reports. No behaviour management plans. No record that Steven has had bananas, grapes and satsumas 542 times for breakfast.

Now, you tell me – who in social services is going to believe that story!

Playing Games With The Vulnerable

September 1, 2012

It's been a long time since I get unduly bothered about the reaction of people to Steven having a meltdown or just being Steven when we are out and about. Unfortunately though, and it's one of the legacies of 2010, I still get very wary of how the professionals will spin Steven's behaviour and general reaction to stuff for their own self-serving ends.

Yesterday, Steven had his six monthly appointment with the psychiatrist. I'd always been fairly ambivalent to his input until he was commissioned to perform Steven's mental capacity assessment whilst he was at the positive behaviour unit. When we received the social work records prior to the court hearing, I saw the referral letter from the social worker to the psychiatrist and it couldn't have been more biased towards the outcome that she wanted. The assessment itself, all 90 minutes of it, consisted of Steven repeatedly saying that he wanted to live in the Uxbridge house. Sadly, the 22 occasions Steven stated his need (I got one of the support workers to count it using a five bar gate system) were never recorded on the final report, which predictably concluded that Steven lacked the capacity to decide where he wanted to live.

Fast forward to the latest appointment. This psychiatrist is a games player and refuses to shake Steven's hand on greeting. This really confuses Steven as his understanding is that whenever he meets someone he knows, he offers his hand and asks for a handshake. The psychiatrist won't even acknowledge the request: he sits thumbing through his notes. Sometimes, in his confusion, Steven gets distressed by this refusal; sometimes he is able to take it in his stride. His distress seems to please the psychiatrist; he becomes more attentive and makes copious notes.

Not knowing how Steven is going to respond to this manipulative bollocks, I get pretty anxious before I've even walked into the room. How is Steven's confusion and possible distress likely to be interpreted and recorded? And then what will Hillingdon's psychologist and the positive behaviour team make of his report? A few years back, after the psychiatrist refused a handshake seven times, Steven got so upset he picked up a file that was sitting on the desk and threw it across the room. That incident was reported as "uncontrollable behaviour" and myself and the support worker "unable to set clear boundaries". See what I mean – its dark stuff.

I have asked the psychiatrist several times if he wouldn't mind shaking Steven's hand but he then tries on the games with me: "It looks like the conflict increases your anxiety Mr Neary". We've tried to explain to Steven that Dr S doesn't shake hands, which he seems to understand as we prepare him for an appointment but upon arrival, hand shaking becomes a reflex action to him. Foolishly once I said that Dr S doesn't shake hands as he has a sore scab on his hand. That made it worse as Steven was then determined to examine the scab.

Apart from that, we are in and out of the door in 15 minutes. It's the same thing every time. Medication? Tick. Behaviour? Tick. Sleeping? Tick. Appetite? Tick. See you in six months. Steven, a support worker and a dad that is wet through with nervous sweat sidle out of the room.

Sad how some people get their sport.

None the Wiser

September 11, 2012

Today was the day for the FACE assessment. I had been sent all the paperwork beforehand but it was so dense that I put it to one side about half way through and never got back to it again.

I like the social worker enormously. She is very straight forward and never uses that "I'm acting in Steven's best interests" line. And the fact that she never says it demonstrates to me that she really is acting in his best interests. If only she had been on our case back in 2010, the whole sorry year would probably never have happened. But instead we were saddled with Mrs Narcissus and the rest, they say, is history.

The first five minutes were odd but cool. SW announced that the assessment as it stands doesn't take into account the following: the need for extra support as a result of challenging behaviour; the need for respite; the need and provision of transport. The assessment tool is currently going through many adaptations and they hope to include these three requirements in future versions. I was gobsmacked. Those three things are Steven's care package! Those three things are his only real needs but the FACE assessment doesn't accommodate any of them. I say it was cool because at least it was up-front and I knew where I stood from the outset. I can't express what a relief that was. None of this "promoting independence" and "facilitating choice" nonsense. The message didn't sound very hopeful but at least it was clear.

What became obvious after about five minutes of questions was that this was an off the peg assessment tool, that is being used in the same state that it was bought. I would hazard a guess and say that if these tools come in several levels of complexity, this was probably the most basic, cheapest model. It was one of those "lets score everything from a value of 0-5" type of tests. And the same rating covers everything from managing money, wiping bottoms, choosing clothes to working the remote control. I'm hopeless at those sort of things; I try to look as if I'm giving each question deep, considered thought but my mind is really wandering off to Leeds' chances of automatic promotion this year. An hour later, we've done as much as we can for today. Most of the questions weren't applicable to Steven (I found the assessment tool was much more geared to the physically disabled than learning disabled) but it was a start. SW promised to write it up what we've done and then we can have another bash at it once the new versions are available (hopefully with questions that might reflect Steven's actual needs).

She also prepared me for the outcome. Because so much of Steven's care package isn't recognised by the assessment, the RAS is likely going to throw out an inappropriately low indicative budget. At the moment his care package has three elements to it:

1. Provision of 2:1 support when Steven is out on an activity and 1:1 support at home whilst I'm at work and for early morning and evening bath.

2. 42 nights a year respite paid via direct payments so I can pay someone to stay overnight whilst I go out.

3. Transport to the activities that aren't within walking distance and would require bus travel.

None of those three needs will be picked up by the RAS. But all is not lost. Whatever indicative budget is revealed, we can then go to the Panel to consider increasing the IB to include the specific needs. Exactly what happens at present but without the costly RAS system acting as the middle man.

There also tentative talk about how I'd like to receive the budget and once again, I kinda switched off but I think there are two options: I can have the whole lot on a pre-paid card or I can directly commission the services myself. At the moment, I don't get involved in the payments to the support agency or the transport firm – I just get direct payments to cover one worker and the respite. So, it sounds like there could be an awful lot more work involved for me.

I left the civic centre and bumped into a friend. I gave her a blow-by-blow account of the proceedings and her response was: "You sound remarkably chipper over something that seems fraught with danger". And she was right. And I'm sure it was because it was all dealt with so honestly, which was astonishingly refreshing. I may lose the 2:1 support, the respite and Steven will be stuck at home because the transport is cancelled, but I do know where I stand. Or perhaps I was still a bit pissed from my respite night last night.

Sudden Endings

September 15, 2012

I've been reflecting on the events of the last four days and trying to work out what the hell was it all about. In less than 48 hours, I swung from terrible despair and fear to triumphant relief and for what? If anyone from the social care field is reading this post, I would genuinely be interested in your theories of how things can change so dramatically, and so suddenly.

A thought struck me this afternoon – this isn't the first time this happened. Not by a long chalk. So much so, that one might almost term it a pattern in my dealings with Hillingdon council. We'll be plodding along and then all of sudden, whoomph, something important to Steven's support system is withdrawn with immediate effect.

Here are five occasions in the past two years:

1. March 2010. Steven had been at the positive behaviour unit for three months. Late one Friday afternoon I received a call from Steven's social worker, informing me that they had implemented a change that would have an immediate impact. They were withdrawing Steven's direct payment package. The next payment was due to go into the account the following Monday morning and I was given 1 working day's notice that it has stopped. The consequences could have been dire. At the time, our direct payment worker who had worked with Steven for 5 years was working about 30 hours per week. He was a vital cog in Steven's life, especially stabilising as a familiar face whilst Steven was struggling to cope with all the changes brought about by the move to the positive behaviour unit. If Hillingdon had got their way, the direct payment worker would have had to be immediately laid off and Steven would have been stuck for his activities on the Monday morning. As it happened, I had a bit of spare money in the direct payment account to continue paying him for a further two weeks. I also, used the money I had put aside to pay the DP tax bill to cover his wages for another two weeks after that. Because he is a loyal man with great integrity, he then did a further two weeks voluntarily. One day, about four weeks after the social worker phoned me, she arrived at my flat unexpectedly just as I was paying his wages. "What's HE doing here?" she said. When I explained, I could see that she was cross and confused that it was inconceivable to her that someone might continue to work unpaid out of loyalty and a strong work ethic. It took six weeks to resolve the issue but

eventually the direct payments were reinstated and backdated to the day they had suddenly stopped. No explanation. No Apology.

2. April 2010. I've written about this many times but the day after Steven made his first escape from the positive behaviour unit, all his daily activities were cancelled with immediate effect, pending risk assessments on all the venues. He was really distressed by this and obviously, couldn't understand why he was being punished in this way. I don't blame him; I didn't understand it either. It took three and a half months for his community programme to be reinstated. They could only carry out one risk assessment a fortnight but ultimately, when the programme was back in place nothing had changed – he was doing exactly the same things at the same places as he had 14 weeks previously.

3. March 2011 and a week before Steven's 21st birthday. Yet again it was a Friday and I was called urgently to a meeting with the social worker to be told they were cancelling the contract with the agency that provides the bulk of Steven's support immediately. It was all very vague with mutterings about "employment irregularities" and "possible immigration issues". This hadn't arisen from a council investigation but from an anonymous tip-off! I contacted Steven's barrister (we were mid trials don't forget at this time) who was an immigration expert and she arranged to see all the workers and the managers at her chambers on the Monday morning. Needless to say, all the papers were in order but it was three weeks before the council reinstated the contract. No explanation. No apology. I had to take three weeks off work as I only had our direct payment worker to cover. The guys were great though and made sure that Steven's birthday plans weren't ruined by working for as much I could get together to pay them out of my pocket. And three weeks after the contract was abruptly cancelled, everything was back in place exactly as it had been before.

4. February 2012 and the saga of the respite package. Hillingdon had spent over a year on different programmes trying to get Steven to return to the centre he used to go to for respite and the same place that he was whipped away from after one night and taken to the positive behaviour unit. These programmes included: desensitising therapy games; subliminal messaging; social story books. None of them worked because he was dead against going back there. For ten months I did without any respite at all and then they agreed to fund a support worker staying overnight at our flat once a fortnight. This worked a treat but then all of a sudden I was notified, guess when, on a Friday, that the respite was being stopped straightaway. I had arranged a night out with a friend for the Saturday which I had to cancel. Three weeks later and

after some intervention from my solicitor the respite was back. For over a year I had been proposing a very cheap respite option and each time it was rejected. Now, all of a sudden it was agreed and respite was back on. No explanation. No Apology. Some of you may remember that this story had a sting in the tail. The week I was due the first direct payment to cover the respite, Hillingdon suddenly deducted a backdated charge for Steven's care from the payment leaving me with 16p to fund the respite. Again it took another solicitor's letter and they admitted the charge was in error and refunded what they had deducted in error.

5. September 2012 and the sudden cancellation of our Housing benefit only for it to be reinstated 48 hours later, during a radio phone in programme!

I'm often challenged by council officers about trust issues. There are several of them that I totally trust and there are lots that I wouldn't trust as far as I could throw them (as Middlesex county boy's discus silver medallist 1976, I could probably throw the shorter ones quite a distance). What I find almost impossible to trust is that this kind of thing won't happen again. It's happened five times now and the consequences have been awful. I don't want to suggest that the intention was to destabilise but that was the outcome of each of these sudden withdrawals. Thankfully, I know Steven well and have excellent support workers, so any destabilising was kept to a minimum.

What I'd like to know is, is this pretty common practice across the country or have I just been unlucky?

Hillingdon's Revenge?

As I write earlier, Steven and I are facing the prospect of becoming homeless. A month after Steven's damages were awarded, a whole series of events happened where Hillingdon have blocked any opportunity we have to secure housing. Their motto could be: "As one door closes, another one closes".

For a while it has felt like Groundhog Day; we are back in 2010 again. It started up another load of media interest and interviews and the legal team are back on board.

I apologies if this section starts to sound repetitious. I did consider summing up the events of the past seven months in one post. But I decided to stick with my original premise and have used every post I have written on the subject. I hope, by doing that, it shows what a horrible, time consuming, stressful time this has been:

- Pay back Time
- U Turn Time
- Rocks & Hard Places
- Eviction Notice
- Heart
- Getting Steven Away
- Just Supposing
- Turning A Deaf Ear
- Love, Belief & Punctured Balls
- A Sheepish Return
- Living In A Box

Pay Back Time?

September 12, 2012

Today I received the shattering news that the housing benefit we have relied on for the last three years to help towards the rent has been stopped by Hillingdon. Ironically, I was notified at a meeting I attended after applying for a discretionary housing payment as I have been really struggling to pay the rent since the rent cap was introduced. The guy admitted that the regulations haven't changed and our circumstances haven't changed but Hillingdon have decided to reinterpret the regulations. They now see our old marital home differently than they have for the past three years. Up until now, they have disregarded the property as not being available to me, as Steven's mother still lives there and is unwilling to sell, and that it is in Steven's best interests to be living away from there. Today, they say that they have to take half the value of the house into account as being available to me and that disqualifies me from any benefit.

So, from October 16th, Steven and I will be homeless. Or there's a possibility that he won't be but we won't be able to live together. Steven could be offered a place under the independent living scheme with 24 hour live in support, possibly even the flat we're currently living in, if I can get the landlord to agree to change the tenancy. But being family, I cannot be that live in support as my presence wouldn't make it "independent". As there is nowhere locally that I could afford to rent on my income, that seems to be the only option open to us, even though it is hardly in Steven's best interests and goes against all the court recommendations. Obviously, the council don't have any duty to rehouse me as a single man, and if I remain as the main applicant, Steven is only treated as a non dependent and his specific needs become irrelevant.

My friend and our solicitor reckon this is Hillingdon's revenge. I don't want to appear too paranoid but it is odd that after three years, their decision about the HB is suddenly completely reversed. In applying for the discretionary payment, I had to lay myself totally bare, so they would be fully aware that it is impossible for Steven and I to live together, anywhere in the borough, without the assistance of the benefit. I wouldn't be able to work more hours to try to make up the shortfall because I don't have the support to cover. In fact, after yesterday's blog about the FACE assessment and the probable outcome of that, I would probably have to reduce my working hours. And the damages that Hillingdon were ordered by the court to pay Steven can be clawed back by Hillingdon from Steven if he becomes the tenant to cover his rent because he will fall into the same category as me as having "funds available". It feels like 2010 all over again because whatever best interests argument I put, and heaven knows, I've got all those expert witness reports that state categorically that Steven should be in his own home with me, Hillingdon can just shrug their shoulders and fell back "on the regulations".

Linda Saunders, our old friend from 2010, is not only director of adult social care but of housing as well, so I've considered appealing to her, whilst remembering that she authorised the "sorry" press release that sought to destroy Steven.

Under housing law, a council has no obligation to house someone if they deem you have made yourself "=intentionally homeless"; I don;t know that there is anything in law to cover the situation where the council intentionally makes you homeless. It feels like I'm in an old western movie and am being driven out-of-town!

I'm tired, very tired but it feels like a race against the clock to get something sorted for Steven before the 16th October. And then his life will really be in the lap of the gods, or in the lap of the Hillingdon gods. A friend just text me to say: "you've got to get away from this persecution". I know it's a strong word but that is exactly what this last two days feels like.

U Turn Time?

September 14, 2012

What an astonishing two days. If I didn't know what a head fuck was before today, I do now.

Yesterday, I was still despairing over the decision by Hillingdon to terminate our Housing Benefit with immediate effect. Then the angels stepped in:

On my five-minute walk from home to the bus stop, three angels appeared. Firstly, I bumped into one of our former local councillor's Wally Kennedy who was so supportive. Then I took a call from Anna Raccoon who has been there in our corner from the beginning and she agreed to write about the latest bombshell. Then, on the bus, Ben Conroy, our solicitor from last year phoned, having read my blog and said he would represent us immediately.

I had a gap at work around lunchtime and my old friend, Billy Kenber from The Times called and we did an interview over the phone. He promised the piece would go in today's paper.

The response to my blog was phenomenal. In 24 hours, it had received 3180 views and all sorts of people were contacting me to offer advice. The great old gang from the Get Steven Home group turned out in force and I find their support really moving and inspirational. Good chats with my great friends, VJ and Ian also helped me clear my head.

This morning I was doing the early morning shop at Sainsburys and took a call from Radio London, inviting me on the Paul Ross and Gaby Roslin show at 8.40. They had interviewed me before, so I knew they would treat the matter fairly. Paul did a great introduction and got me to explain what happened on Wednesday. He quickly started to pursue the possibility that there may be a connection between the abrupt cessation of my claim and the recent award of damages. And then Linda Saunders, the director of social care and housing at Hillingdon came on. She said that she had personally intervened in the case this morning and had reinstated the HB whilst further discussions took place. I have been invited to a meeting on Tuesday to look at what options are available. It was an astonishing u turn in just two days. Paul came back to me for a response and I just said that I was gobsmacked but it was fantastic news.

What on earth have the last two days been about?

Rocks and Hard Places

September 24, 2012

So, a quick update on the "ongoing discussions" about my housing benefit problem. The clock is ticking towards the 16th October and it still feels a million miles away from resolution.

I had the first of the meetings with the professionals: a social care manager; a housing benefit manager and a housing manager. They confirmed that the decision to end the housing benefit was correct on the grounds that although their regulations state that the capital from a second property can be disregarded in full if it is occupied by an incapacitated relative (it is – Steven's mother has paranoid schizophrenia); the regulations do not classify a "wife" as a relative. They acknowledged that Steven cannot live in the marital home and I had a terrible Hobson's choice back in 2009 – care for Steven or care for my wife, but they cannot "break the law by bending the regulations". I did remind them about the court judgement from 2011 where Justice Jackson quoted a senior manager as saying (about the deprivation of liberty authorizations): " we are acting legally on everyone's behalf" and this situation had a familiar feel to it, but to no avail.

I was given two options:

1. Persuade my landlady to transfer the tenancy into Steven's name. Even if she agrees to that, there are several difficulties. Firstly, they said Steven would have to undergo yet another mental capacity assessment to determine if he has the capacity to become a tenant. (We're still waiting for the mental capacity assessment about whether he can manage finances before we get the damages claim). But far more threatening, they said that if Steven became the tenant, they would have to take his damages into account as capital available to him and that would disqualify him from housing benefit. So, that would put him in exactly the same position as me. One of the officers mentioned putting the money into trust for him (which is what I'm planning to do if we ever get the money) but another officer said they might still have to disqualify him because it could be argued that the capital had been deliberately disposed of in order to obtain benefit.

2. We move back to the marital home and try to force Steven's mother to leave (or swap properties with her). That might work if, a, she was willing

(she's not) and, b, she had the capacity to make the decision (she hasn't). And try selling a house with someone refusing to move!

Even though it goes against all the expert witnesses recommendations that it is overwhelmingly in Steven's best interests to live in his own home with me and that any move would have a major negative effect on his well-being, mental state and behaviour, we also discussed Steven having to go into care if no resolution can be found. But of course, even though that is the last thing that both he or I would want, they would still treat him as if he was a tenant and still get back his damages by charging him.

I'd like to be able to work more and not have this terrible dependency. At the moment I work about 24 hours a week in my counselling practice. I could get a second job somewhere and solve the problem but I don't have (and wouldn't get) the support to care for Steven to enable me to do that.

Tricky, eh?

Eviction Notice

November 13, 2012

It's been an awful day and I do feel like I'm reaching the end of my fighting capacity (There's a thought – perhaps if you're engaged in dealings with your local authority, you should have a fighting capacity assessment!). This morning I received the shocking news about my Housing Benefit. This afternoon, I passed out – I'm sure it was the stress of the latest bombshell, but it was scary nonetheless.

Today I was called to meet the people from the housing department about my housing benefit claim. To recap, for people who haven't read the earlier blogs on the subject, I have been getting Housing benefit continuously since we moved to this flat in 2009. In July, I asked for my claim to be reassessed as my income had gone down a fair bit since I went out on my own in my own practice. I went along for a meeting, which I thought was to be about the reassessment, only to be told that they had looked at my claim again and that I was no longer entitled to HB. The reason they gave was that I jointly own the home that Steven's unwell mother lives in and their position is that I have access to the funds of that property. I don't – his mother is very ill and cannot sell the property. That has always been the case since 2009 and I checked out that very point before we took up this tenancy. I was informed at the first meeting that they were stopping the Housing Benefit with immediate effect. The following day I got in touch with all the press contacts I made during the court case in 2011 and The Times and the local paper ran the story. I was also invited onto Radio London and was interviewed by Paul Ross. Astonishingly, mid interview, Linda Saunders, the director of Housing came on air and said that she had personally intervened and was reinstating the benefit whilst further discussions took place. That was two months ago and the benefit has remained paid since. I went to one meeting, the week after the radio interview, and was given 2 options to think about. I had already taken legal advice, which was that we had a very good case, so not to consider the other options and appeal the decision to stop the HB. I submitted the appeal on 26th September. I have heard nothing until today.

It felt like Groundhog Day. It came out in court that all the discussions between the LA and me over Steven's care were "window dressing", whilst they sought legal advice and got their own legal case in order (as we know, that failed dismally). The same thing happened today. The housing officer admitted that the delay of two months has been whilst they sought legal advice. Not as Linda Saunders promised, to have further discussions. They were confident that their decision is legally sound and so are stopping the housing benefit again from 19th November. I said that I have no confidence in their ability to get a legal matter correct after 2010 and wanted to pursue the appeal. Amazingly, they said that my appeal is only valid from today as their formal decision was notified to me today. And the formal decision only states that I am not entitled as "you have capital in excess of £16000". If I want a fuller explanation, I have to request it and that slows down the process even more. That means I will have to go through the charade of an internal appeal (which of course will get nowhere) and then hopefully, to the social security commission. It will take a long time, and in the meantime, I don't have the money to pay the full rent. So, even if the appeal is successful, by then it will be too late – we will already be evicted.

That led us to the other options. The council have no duty to rehouse me as a single man; but they do have a duty towards Steven. However, they won't do anything until we have been evicted from our flat. So, next rent day, I will just have to pay what I can afford and let the landlady serve an eviction notice. Leaving aside, the deep shame of that as I've had a very good relationship with my landlady and have never once missed a payment of rent, they cannot start a rehousing of Steven until eviction is served.

The new property, probably a council flat, will have to be in Steven's name. That throws up two problems. Firstly, I would have to act on his behalf as he lacks capacity to manage a tenancy and we are still waiting for the court of protection date for my welfare deputyship application. I checked with the lawyer this morning to make sure that the application we have submitted will cover me having to oversee the tenancy on his behalf. The second kick in the balls is that Steven wouldn't qualify for housing benefit either because of his compensation. I said that we haven't received it yet and that the court will hold on to it until I become the welfare deputy, but their opinion is that because they have released the funds, it is available to Steven. So, despite the assurances from Linda Saunders and regardless of whether it was their intention, they will indirectly get the money back that the court ordered them to pay as compensation for their illegal act. The rent will probably be significantly cheaper than the private rent I pay at the moment, but the outcome is still the same; whether Steven or I are the tenant, neither of us will get any help towards the rent. The place will have to be furnished, so another chunk of his compensation will have to go on that. The poor sod is likely to have very little left of his damages by this time next year. I've had to completely revise my ideas that the damages would pay for him to have some good holidays over the next few years.

Of course, Steven's best interests didn't enter into the conversation once; neither did the recommendations of the court experts.

So, add today's news with the situation from yesterday's blog about the long-term sickness of the direct payment worker and how do I fund his sick pay and a replacement worker. Throw into the pot, the fact that we are still waiting for the damages payout 18 months after the court case and it all feels very bleak right now.

No final joke today – I think the joke is on me.

Heart

November 14, 2012

This is a quick update as it's another full on day and I need to get some rest as well.

Last night I ended up in A&E. I'm sure it was the stress of the day. It's funny how being wired up to a heart monitor clears the brain. And a very odd thing happened. One of the nurses was asking me what had happened and it turned out she'd read my book. She made a very good observation: "Funny how on both times you've asked for help from Hillingdon, it's turned into a nightmare".

She was right. But it's helped me decide on the approach today when I meet the housing officer to discuss the step by step process of the eviction and rehousing.

Hillingdon have never understood families and the importance of family life (if anything they are quite hostile towards it), so why bother trying to discuss on those terms. There is no point in getting into a moral, humanitarian, ethical discussion about the situation either – they don't work on that level. The only way this will work is to work on the lowest common denominator – their duty of care towards Steven.

So, take me out of the picture; I am just a live in carer – I am as relevant as one of the support workers. The focus has to be on Steven's place of residence.

That leaves a simple choice. Stay here in our flat or move to social housing. As Steven will be expected to pay the full rent as they will exclude him from HB because of his damages, what will work best for Steven? So, it boils down to what will preserve his compensation the longer, and that will be social housing.

I want to thank all the people who have messaged me on this blog, Twitter and Facebook since yesterday with advice and suggestions on people who can intervene. I really do appreciate it. I'm too tired and unwell at the moment to act on those suggestions but I will get on to it as soon as I feel better.

Getting Steven Away

November 16, 2012

On Wednesday, I attended the second meeting to look at our housing options with two senior managers from Hillingdon; one from housing and one from social care. (Cost to me over the two days £120 in lost earnings). Surprisingly, the option of social housing that the deputy director of housing had suggested the day before had suddenly disappeared off the table. That despite Hillingdon giving a statement to the BBC an hour before the meeting saying that the social housing option could be the most favourable option.

Three options were presented:

1. We move back to the marital home with no rental liability. The consequences of that though (which the social care manager acknowledged may happen) is that social services would immediately raise a safeguarding adults alert on Steven and probably within a short space of time, would remove Steven from my care. That is exactly the same position we were in back in 2009 which prompted us leaving the family home. Also, it would be impossible to sustain a care package in that environment.

2. I meet the full rental liability myself. I'd love to be able to do that and get away from the benefits system and trying to increase my income isn't for the want of trying. However, the stumbling block with this option is that if I did find more work, I don't have the support in place to enable me to work more hours. Social services have made it very clear that they will not increase the support package.

3. Hillingdon will make up the shortfall in my rent from their discretionary homeless fund. This would be a very temporary arrangement and is conditional. The condition is that once we have been to the Court of Protection (looking like the end of January now) and I am appointed Steven's welfare deputy, Hillingdon would expect me to transfer the tenancy into Steven's name. As he wouldn't be entitled to housing benefit either, by virtue of his damages, he would have to pay the full rental liability out of his damages. I'm not convinced that is legally sound but even if it is, it is morally and ethically vile. Obviously, I would still pay as much as I can towards the rent but his damages would still disappear very quickly.

I have asked Steven's legal team to consider three things (and if anyone reading this knows the answers, please get in touch because I would be very grateful):

1. Is Hillingdon's decision to stop my housing benefit legally correct? I have appealed but unfortunately because of how Hillingdon have orchestrated it, time is against us, so we'll be served an eviction notice before the appeal is heard.

2. Is there a way of protecting Steven's damages, so he doesn't end up having to pay the full rent?

3. Is it legal for me to be appointed welfare deputy and then the next day, transfer my tenancy into Steven's name and lumbering him with a £950 a month rental liability?

Here's the news. I think the best thing to do is to move right away from Hillingdon. This relentless harassment has continued for five years now and even if this latest issue gets sorted favourably, there will be something else around the corner. There always is. I've been looking into the option of shared ownership and could use a large chunk of Steven's damages to really secure his accommodation for the future. I've been looking at Kent as I have some friends there already and there is even the possibility that a couple of Steven's support workers would still be able to work with him. There are other options I can consider but perhaps now is the time, having got Steven home, to get him away from Hillingdon for good.

Just Supposing……..

November 18, 2012

I received a direct message on Facebook earlier from someone who has read the recent blogs and asked me: "Just supposing Hillingdon have got it terribly wrong again. The appeal commission could decide that you were entitled to housing benefit all along but by that time, you will be evicted from your home. What will happen to Hillingdon after a second unlawful act in two years….."

I've just typed up the chronology of my housing benefit history for my solicitor and thought I'd post it here. As you can see, since the 12th September, there have been several occasions where my right to appeal has been jeopardized, now resulting in the probability of being evicted before an appeal is even heard.

Chronology of Housing Benefit Claim

July 2009	Informed by social worker that it is impossible to sustain support package due to wife's mental health state. Unless something changes, Steven could be removed from my care.
August 2009	I find flat in Uxbridge and check with Housing Benefit department about eligibility to claim before signing tenancy agreement. Given the all clear by HB department. Social worker writes letter to HB to support the move.
16th August 2009	Steven and I move into flat in Uxbridge
August 2009 to September 2012	Housing Benefit paid continuously. Several reassessments of claim during this period, including discretionary award in September 2011.
28th August 2012	I ask for HB claim to be reassessed as my income has decreased, following change in employment.
12th September 2012	Meet with HB officer. Discuss my income details. Am informed that HB is terminated due to situation with marital home. Formal termination letter issued by Hillingdon
14th September 2012	Director of Housing states on radio programme that she has reinstated the HB "whilst ongoing discussions take place". I receive email from social care manager confirming the reinstatement and advising me to ignore the termination letter of 12th

18th September 2012	I meet with managers from HB, Housing & Social Care. I wish to challenge decision to terminate HB but focus of meeting on options open to me after the termination.
25th September 2012	I submit social security commissioner's decision to support my claim. No acknowledgement
26th September 2012	I submit formal appeal against decision to terminate HB. No acknowledgement.
4th October 2012	Receive the minutes of the meeting of 12th September. Appeal not acknowledged.
5th October to 12th November 2012	No communication.
13th November 2012	Attend meeting with HB manager, Social care manager & Deputy director of Housing. Given formal letter that HB is terminated from 19th November. Told that my previous appeal not valid until today. Delay and lack of communication since 4th October because Hillingdon seeking legal advice.
14th November 2012	Attend meeting with Housing manager & social care manager. Am presented with several options, all based on there being no HB

As to the question what will happen to Hillingdon – the answer is probably nothing whatsoever!

Turning A Deaf Ear

January 31, 2013

It's been over five months since I was informed that the LA were stopping my housing benefit, and by God, has it been a long five months. The lack of activity and the awful feeling of being trapped and powerless has been doing my head in.

Last week I received the sealed court order appointing me as Steven's property and affairs deputy. The order is very clear that if I have a conflict of interests over any decision for Steven, an IMCA needs to be appointed or the court has to make the decision. Hillingdon's preferred plan is that I transfer the tenancy into Steven's name and he uses his damages award to meet the rental liability. As I have an obvious conflict of interests with this plan, any decision has to be a best interest's decision for Steven. I have asked Hillingdon repeatedly for an IMCA referral but they are again doing what Justice Jackson criticised them for – turning a deaf ear. I haven't even had my requests acknowledged; let alone acted on. Sorry for sounding like a cracked record but the sooner people can contact the IMCA service directly and not have to rely on an LA referral, the better. I've tried to kick start the best interests process. As the deputy, and presumably the RPR, I've contributed my own best interest's assessment, but like the request for and IMCA, that has been ignored too.

Hillingdon have neatly stitched up relations with my landlady. They insisted they had to contact her to inform her about the change in rent payments and since then, she's adopted the deaf ear approach too. I can guess what is happening. Having got wind of us probably being evicted, the landlady is hoping to hold on to our deposit when we go and use our money, rather than her own to carry out the repairs in readiness for the next tenant. So, at the moment, we have a dangerous temporary wiring in the fuse box; a leaky radiator causing horrible damage to the flat downstairs; broken floor tiles in the bathroom that we keep cutting our feet on; a broken bed; a broken sofa and a boiler that alarmingly keeps flashing its warning light. I wish this council were as keen to risk assess the property as they are to risk assess Steven.

I'd love to move. I am quite comfortable that a move would be in Steven's best interests and would give him long term security. I'm comfortable using some of his damages to enable him to have this security. Ah – the damages! 19 months on, we're still waiting for them. The latest news is that, despite two court orders about costs, the solicitor wants to double – check with the Legal

Services Commission in case any costs need to be deducted from the award. I've actually got to the point where I don't believe Steven will ever get his damages award.

I've written before about systems and being caught up in so many systems is exhausting. If I'm truly honest, I haven't met one system that can honestly say they are acting in the best interests of the person they are serving. I've had a lot of faith in the legal system but the latest delay in releasing the damages is extremely disappointing. I've asked several times for a tiny proportion of them so that I can buy Steven a new bed but am told sympathetically that there is a process to go through.

Processes. Systems. Best interests. For whom?

Love Belief & Punctured Balls

February 27, 2013

This is my last blog post on Love, Belief and Balls. I had my latest meeting with Hillingdon today about our housing situation and the cards on the table were, quite frankly, shite.

My number one goal in life ever since Steven came along has been to provide him with the best possible quality of life I can help him achieve. I've always known that when I'm no longer around, his future is going to be very bleak and that has increased the pressure and my desire to the best for him whilst he still has me around to love and care for him and to fight his corner for him. The latest battle to secure a home for him has been one fight too many and in my view, I have lost. And I cannot continue to write about our life, about social justice whilst I carry the guilt of having failed him so miserably. In spite of the High Court ruling and the evidence of the very good home life he leads at the moment, nothing can be done to stop Hillingdon's vindictiveness. In short, I can't protect him any longer from the people who are meant to responsible for his care.

In July, when our tenancy expires, Hillingdon will have received the authority to make Steven the tenant, whether it is at our current flat or another private rented property. They have already started that ball rolling and time is too short, and a fight too costly to stop the ball.

All the other options are off the table:

- If we move back to the marital home, Steven will be taken into care.

- If I try to sell the marital home, the estimate from the legal people is that it would take at least two years to sell because of my wife's incapacity. It will be very expensive to sell because of the large court costs that would be run up trying to evict an incapacitated person from her home. And in that time, we would be made homeless anyway.

- I can try and find a second job so I won't be reliant on housing benefit to pay part of the rent but the council won't increase my support package. I don't have enough hours in the week when I'm not caring for Steven on my own to get another job.

- They won't consider Steven for social housing because his damages award exceeds their £30,000 eligibility policy. If I spend some of it or put it in a trust fund, they will deem that I have disposed of his capital to secure him a tenancy and take it into account anyway. Even if I use the money in a manner that they approve of, Steven would still have to join a long waiting list and either be in care or bed and breakfast in the meantime. In short, Hillingdon believes that it's housing allocation policy trumps it's duty of care towards Steven (and also trumps the High Court best interests' judgement).

So, that leaves us with Steven going into care or becoming a private tenant. The latter is preferable for his quality of life but it would mean that all his damages will be used up within two years in paying rent.

I'd love a judicial review of the whole sorry story. I'd love to go back before Justice Peter Jackson and see what he has to say about Hillingdon's shameful actions. But I can't afford that. And that's why I can't write about this stuff anymore. I can't look myself or Steven in the eye because I feel so hopelessly ashamed. I remember one writer, after the court case, described it as a "David & Goliath story". That's bollocks really. In real life, Goliath usually wins.

A Sheepish Return

March 2, 2013

Erm …… Is it okay to come back in?

Thursday and Friday in Leeds for the Best Interests Assessor's Conference were two very crazy days. I've often said that angels crop up in the most unlikely of places. But the trick is being able to see and hear the angels when they appear and not to be blinded by cynicism or depression when they appear. So, with that in mind, I'd like to thank from the bottom of my heart, the following angels who arrived over the last two days. In order of appearance: Victoria Derbyshire, Ben Conroy, Hazel, My Sister Jayne, Luke, Derek, Yvonne and the all the good folk from the Yorkshire and Humber BIA conference, Ian and Val. You've all pulled me back from a very dark place.

I arrived in Leeds mid afternoon on Thursday, exhausted and in a black hole. I found myself bursting into tears on Kings Cross Station when I discovered I'd missed the train by five minutes. It didn't matter that another one was departing in 20 minutes; I fed it into the malaise that I'd felt since the meeting with Hillingdon on Wednesday. Throughout Thursday, I tried to do all sorts of things to chill me out but none of them worked (I was having to deal with my landlady and the leaking radiator most of the day!). I had an hour in the spa pool in the hotel but unusually, I came out more stressed than when I went in. I had a lovely meal in the restaurant but I couldn't finish it. I took some of my favourite DVDS with me but didn't get more than five minutes into them. I went to the bar and had a pint and tried to read my Barry Cryer (one of my heroes) book but couldn't even finish my pint. I retired to bed with Question Time on and found myself getting seriously worked up by the terrible Tory woman on the panel. Probably too much detail, but I couldn't even have a wank! I must have fallen to sleep about 12.30.

I was woken up on Friday morning by my phone ringing and it was the Victoria Derbyshire show on Radio Five Live. They had read my last blog post and Victoria wanted to interview me. I've been interviewed by Victoria three times previously but I felt nervous about accepting. I didn't want to piss off Hillingdon any more but then thought there was nothing I could say that would make our relationship any worse than it is. As usual, Victoria was very fair and at one point made me cry by remarking that I sounded very weary. It lasted about 15 minutes and I was gobsmacked when I heard the show back on I Player – they hadn't edited the interview at all and I had been given the whole

15 minutes aired. It was only 8.30 am and I did the whole interview in my pants sitting on the edge of the bed in my hotel room. Thank you Victoria – I think she recognises our story as symbolic of a lot of what is wrong with the social care field and what happens when power is abused so cynically.

By the time I dressed and went downstairs, the delegates were arriving but I had to miss the first session as my solicitor from 2011, Ben Conroy had set up a conference call to discuss the housing problem. I'd had to check out by this time, so I had to find a quiet space in this busy hotel. I ended up in a corridor by the spa pool. Ben is great – very direct and it's pow pow pow – this is what we have to do. By the end of a fifteen minute phone conversation we had worked out an action plan that hopefully will answer whether the actions of Hillingdon in the three big issues (stopping my HB, forcing Steven to become the tenant and blocking him from social housing) are illegal.

The conference was now well underway and as I made my way to the main hall, I met Hazel. Hazel is not a BIA or an AMHP; she is a parent like me. She introduced me to her son who looked remarkably like Steven. Hazel is from the Get Steven Home group and she told me how she had been in a similar situation to us and had a long battle to get her son home. I got choked up when she told me that she had travelled across Yorkshire to hear me speak. For the first time since the group started in July 2010, I met someone who had been a supporter from afar. It was ever so heartening.

During all this, I was taking phone calls from my sister Jayne, who was trying to sort out a plumber for my radiator back home. As well as succeeding in that mission, she also announced that she had found me a potential flat. And the best thing about it was that it was away from Hillingdon but so near as to not affect my work, Steven's activities or his support. I had never considered moving to the next county before; I'd never realised that the borders of that county are so close to where we currently live. Wouldn't that be magnificent – to one day announce to Hillingdon that we're moving away. (When I got home, I discovered that the flat had gone but it has sowed a seed and I am definitely going to pursue this option). She's great, my sister. Whenever I'm in a hard place; she's my rock.

It was time for my Q&A session and they both went really well. Derek and Luke chaired a session each and it was fascinating how interested people were in our story. It was weird how respected I felt by all the people at the conference compared to the way I'd been treated like a piece of shit by Hillingdon two days earlier. Of course, people are always fascinated by the hidden agenda and

I kept being asked what I thought 2010 was really all about. Now that's it all over, I can verbalise my theories and it was interesting that they made a lot of sense to the delegates. We had a discussion about the abuse of power and I shocked them by telling them the story from Wednesday's meeting. The housing manager was insisting that Steven's damages preclude him from social housing. To illustrate his power, he talked about a young caretaker who had died suddenly leaving a wife and three young children. The council had to evict him from his caretaker's property but then, with pride, the manager announced that they had no duty to house the wife and kids because of the pay out from the staff pension scheme. I didn't think it was a story to be proud of and I'm sure was only told as a cock wagging exercise. It's not pleasant to be involved in this arrogant power wielding. One of the good things about going on the Mark Neary roadshow is that I've now encountered lots of other BIAs and La officials and they have nothing like that sneering attitude of Hillingdon.

I was getting texts from Ian and VJ throughout the day and when I got home and they both know how to drag me out of my black moods. I'm very lucky.

And that was that. Exhausting but after the hell of Wednesday's meeting, I think I found a big bit of heaven again.

And if you don't mind, I think I'll come back.

Living In A Box

March 25, 2013

First the good news. I have found somewhere for Steven and I to live. It's available from mid May and I can afford the rent without having to rely on Housing Benefit. It also means that Steven's compensation money will not have to be used to pay any rent. It's also within about 25 minutes walking distance from my work, so I will save on travelling expenses.

That's the end of the good news. The bad news (and there's quite a bit of it) is that it's only a studio flat. One room and a small kitchen and shower room. It boasts a dressing room but I can't quite see where that fits in. Steven can have the bed which pulls down every night and I'll buy a sofa bed for myself. The room is very pokey, so they'll probably only be room for an armchair, the TV and a storage system for all Steven's DVDs and CDs. I'll flog my DVDs and I'll trade in the PC for a laptop. It's ironic because the whole flat would probably fit into one of the rooms we had at Center Parcs last week.

Goodness knows how we'll manage with the lack of space. I think Steven will find it very difficult. He likes having his own space and that is going to be very hard. We'll have to stop the overnight respite as well because there won't be anywhere for the support worker to sleep. Although to be honest, as a result of the fairer charging policy, it wasn't really worth having the respite – having one night out was costing quite a bit and that's before I even set foot outside the door.

Hillingdon will be pursuing their application to manage a private tenancy on Steven's behalf. I had an interesting conversation with a housing lawyer, who felt it is scandalous, that someone with such high level needs as Steven is being forced into private housing, but that's their local housing policy for you. I'm fascinated to see how they present Steven to potential private landlords in order to secure a tenancy. I guess it will be the complete opposite to 2010. Then, in order to get their way, they had to spin Steven in the worst possible light. Now, they'll have to present him as unproblematic. It doesn't matter; to them the spin is everything.

I think we've got some tough times ahead.

Update 26th March 2013:

I heard back from the landlord of the studio flat today via the estate agents. He will not be offering us the tenancy as he doesn't think the flat is suitable for a disabled person. I don't know whether there's anything discriminatory there but he's right. A studio flat is wildly unsuitable but I haven't got much choice. That's the third place we've been turned down for now – I think the council have really underestimated how difficult it is to get a privately rented property when one of the occupants is LD.

I also had an email from the council – they also think the studio flat is "unsuitable and too limited". No shit Sherlock. They just don't get it. We're only in this horrible position because of their rigid interpretation of the law and their own local housing allocation policies.

The Man Who Uses a Sprinkler Attachment Up His Arse As A Way of Getting Even

Most domestic properties in Feasability Street are bastions of conventionality. What you see is what you get. Bedrooms are used for sleeping and sexual intercourse; lounges are used for flute recitals and crib evenings; bathrooms are used for flossing and blackhead popping. Etc etc.

This trend of conventionality is bucked at number 117 Feasability Street, home to the slightly eccentric, Christian Gimpler-Freud. The whole house has been gutted and was now one vast space; part engineering workshop; part laboratory. There was even a passing resemblance to a dressmaker's studio with the mannequin by the fireplace. Occasionally, one could detect a glimpse of domesticity: a hammock hung in a secluded alcove; a commode in the shape of a giraffe sat discreetly to the left of the bay window. Nobody would have guessed that the commonplace cream cracker tin was actually a working microwave. Even less would people have deduced that the blow up Andrew Lloyd Webber was in reality, a fully functioning tumble drier.

Christian Gimpler-Freud had a passion. Gadgetry. Breath taking invention. And fortunately, due to his father being killed at a stag hunt in 1991, Christian had the funds to indulge his passion. Lord Malcom Gimpler-Freud had been a big cheese in the potted shrimp world and had left his sole heir a considerable fortune. And it wasn't just his late father's money that had come in useful. The late knight's spleen hung majestically from the high ceiling and had been transformed into a splendid smoke alarm.

Mr Gimpler-Freud junior had a few commandments; one of the most notable being that everything has a use – nothing is valueless. Going against his ancestral right wing instincts, Christian believed that there was no difference between a rich man and a poor man. Especially when their scrotum could be hollowed out, glazed and used as a nice pair of egg cups. However, true to his conservative leanings, Christian believed that every man must be responsible for himself and that there was too much self absorbed shilly shallying around these days. And it was with this thought in mind that led him to immerse himself night and day for the past five months in his latest ground breaking novelty.

A casual observer may have suspected that Mr Gimpler-Freud was perilously close to that thin line, which once crossed, inevitably led to a path of self-righteous grandiosity. But pride, self belief and a strong sense of justice had always been a prevailing family trait and Christian was determined to carry on this proud family tradition.

The 31st August 2012 was to be the day the fruits of Christian's labours would be unleashed onto an unsuspecting world. He woke early and had a small toilet. Eager to get cracking, he multi tasked and lubricated his wondrous 18 inch sprinkler attachment whilst tucking into a bowl of multi Cheerios. Replenished and still in his monogrammed dressing gown, Christian disrobed and gingerly inserted the well lubed sprinkler (right end up) into his arsehole. Familiar with bottom play from his days at Eton, it wasn't an entirely unpleasant experience, but the last five inches did induce a rather unexpected gagging reflex. Once in place, Christian screwed on the sprinkler head and familiarised himself one last time with the four important buttons marked: "on/off", "drop flap", "load" and "spray". Resisting the urge of a self satisfied smile, Christian walked to the dressmakers dummy and removed the rather alarming outfit hanging from it. Coming from an engineering background, Christian winced as he regretted paying such scant attention in his needlecraft class. The outfit was part boiler suit; part tuxedo with a cunning zipped flap covering its anal regions. Glancing at himself in the mirror, Christian decided that he could explain away the un-nerving bulge caused by the sprinkler head, as a bad case of haemorrhoids or a medium sized cauliflower incubating. Now, fully suited and booted, Christian was ready to face the day and perhaps discover the opportunity for some high jinks vigilantism.

He didn't have long to wait. His local health centre had six reception booths and as he waited to hand in a repeat prescription for sherbet lemons, he was disturbed to find no receptionists in attendance. Small queues were forming but the six receptionists, all called Barbara, were deep in conference:

"I can nip to Tescos in my coffee break".

"But we can't submit our lottery ticket until Barbara has paid her £5".

"I know your terrapin's birthday is the 30th Barbara but the numbers don't go up that high".

"Barbara – I think it's time we changed number 18. I plump for number23".

Christian and the other 14 people in the queue had become edgy. In fact, Christian was going through a Churchillian moment. Knowing that once started, there would be no turning back, his index finger hovered anxiously over his flap controller pad. His Waterloo moment came when one of the Barbaras dropped her bag of 2ps and all the other Barbaras got down on all fours to pick it up.

Christian pressed the button. Wagner filled the surgery as his bum flap unzipped and twelve inches of sprinkler emerged from his throbbing arse cheeks. He pressed "load" and a diet of spicy foods and full cream products did their business. By now, all eyes were on Christian, except for the six Barbaras who were now comparing nail varnishes. And as Wagner reached a crescendo, our hero pressed "spray".

The impact was instant and glorious. A tsunami of mahogany shade shit exploded into the air. Patient notes were splattered. Stool sample bottles were unexpectedly filled. Prescription pads were sodden in a Daddies sauce hue. And the six Barbaras stood aghast as they resembled the Black and White Minstrels. And as their permed hair trembled, little flakes of turd dropped onto their Euro millions voucher.

His work complete, Christian did one final dump on a small calling card bearing the family crest and handed it to a bemused Dr Clegg who fell out of his consulting room door, having self administered a heroin/martini injection.

All was right with the world again.

Being An Employer & The Support Team

It would be impossible to have any sort of life without the support of our great team of support workers. This section is partly a tribute to them but also what it's like to have a staff in your home. The plusses far outweigh the minuses but there are times when I yearn for some space to myself. I know that Steven sometimes feels the same as well.

And being a carer and asking for a support package means you suddenly become an employer as well, with all the paperwork that entails. So, your time space is limited further by having to do tax returns, pay wages, compile direct payment accounts.

- Working From Home
- I Just Want To be A Dad
- A Delightful Log
- Never Forget – Howard Donald Leaves Our Support Team

Working From Home

July 18, 2012

Last week, I went and visited a friend in their home. Nothing unusual in that, although I realised it was for me. I can't remember the last time I visited someone else's home. I was only there an hour but I became obsessed with how normal their family life was. Whilst I chatted to my friend, other members of her family got on with their homework; mowed the lawn; discussed who would have control of the television viewing from 9pm. My home life is nothing like that.

I want to point out that this post isn't a whinge. My home life couldn't be any other way. I just wanted to present a narrative about what it's like to live in a home that is several other people's workplace.

When Steven first came home from the positive behaviour unit, my solicitor advised me to have support in the home from 6 in the morning to 9 at night, seven days a week. Much of Hillingdon's case against me was based on two assertions: I under report incidents and I am at risk from Steven. Needless to say, they were unable to come up with any evidence to support their beliefs and the judge rightly criticised them for it. But I went along with the solicitor's advice for one simple reason: I am not at risk from Steven but I am at risk from social services. They have never acknowledged that they got those assertions wrong and all their actions since the case lead me to believe that their ongoing input is not about support but about litigating and collecting evidence.

So, what is it like having people around from 6am to 9pm? On the one hand, the guys are incredibly supportive and have made it their mission that they do all the support when they are at work. There are a few times during the week when not a lot is happening as Steven has become so much better at engaging himself, and the support staff will suddenly do my ironing for me, or go round with the hoover. This sounds fantastic, and it is, but sometimes I yearn for the normality of doing a pile of ironing.

I guess it is hard if you are a support worker in someone's home to constantly be aware that it is someone's home and not just your workplace. I get up at 6am to let the support worker in and he takes over and does Steven's breakfast and supports him during his bath. If I haven't got an early start at work, the staff encourages me to go back to bed. I need little encouragement for that but I'm aware that I am trying to sleep in my home, whilst someone else is working in their workplace. A good, but embarrassing example of this is a couple of weeks ago I had gone back to bed and was enjoying a dawn wank when my bedroom door suddenly burst open and the support worker happily brought the washing in to hang up. Apologies all round but an awkward moment to say the least.

I wrote at length last week about the logs I have to keep for Social Services benefit and the symbolism of the big blue binder doesn't escape me. My dining room table that houses the newspapers; bills, Steven's symbols and is used as our place of dining is also someone else's office. Every part of my flat is multipurpose – my home; the support worker's work station. Believe me, this takes some head adjustment and I do struggle with it at times.

Sharing the space with non family members is something that I noticed my friend didn't have to do. My fridge has the support worker's food and drink in it as well as ours'; Steven's wardrobe has the support worker's change of clothes hanging up when they do an overnight; my bedroom chair has the support workers' swimming stuff as they do five swims a week with Steven. It couldn't be any other way but it can feel intrusive.

At 9 o'clock the shutters come down on the workplace and Steven and I have a home to ourselves. In 18 months, nothing that I couldn't cope with has ever happened in that time; in fact, I think Steven really likes the time when he has me all to himself. Last night, Steven went up for bed at his usual time of 9.45pm. We do his "Waltons" routine for 10 minutes and then he was fast asleep. I'd been looking forward all day to going back downstairs after he fell asleep and catching up on my Lewis boxed set. I gathered supplies; a glass of beer and a large bar of Galaxy. I laid my duvet expectantly over the sofa, got myself comfy and them felt a sharp poke in my back: one of the support workers had left his umbrella on the sofa. It actually drew blood. The moment had passed and I came upstairs and started to write this blog.

In all yesterday, I was awake from 6am to 11pm and only had two hours when our home was just a home. And even that two hours was interrupted by a lethal brolley. Home sweet home.

I Just Want To Be A Dad

October 19, 2012

I got home from work today to find a letter from HMRC, informing me that from April 2013, the PAYE paperwork must be submitted every time a payment is made. At the moment, I pay the PAYE every three months and submit the paperwork once a year.

I am resentful of having to be an employer in the first place. I am an employer because I receive a direct payments package to pay a support worker to support my son. I needed help with being a carer and suddenly found myself becoming an employer in the process.

To begin with it wasn't a problem. When we first received direct payments in 2005, the rules allowed the support worker to be self-employed. So, I used to give him a cheque once a month and left him to sort out his own tax and national insurance. Just the way, every other self-employed worker in the country is remunerated for their services. At the time, he was working with Steven for 5 hours a week, so it wasn't an arduous process for either him or me. Somewhere along the way, HMRC decided that direct payment workers should be employed and therefore the parent or carer had to become an employer of the PA. Now that Steven has left school and needs support during the week, our direct payment package is now 36 hours per week and I have two workers sharing those hours. Not a huge workforce or payroll but time-consuming nonetheless.

It takes me two hours a month to do all the paperwork required; not only is there the HMRC paperwork to be completed but the LA want to see the records to and they have a different format for doing them. That may not sound like an awful lot of time, but bear in mind that I only have five hours each week when I'm not caring or working – I can think of a million things I'd rather be doing with that time other than sitting with my calculator and the headfuck that is the HMRC forms.

Employ a payroll company I hear you say – my LA offered to introduce me to one. I don't know what things are like in other parts of the country but the two I approached locally charge for this service and I would be expected to find this payment out of the normal monthly direct payment package. Our package is very tightly calculated by the LA; it works out the exact hours of care Steven needs a week and pays for those hours. There is no slack and if I don't use those 36 hours every week, I cannot save them up for something or use them for something else. If I did, the LA would claim the money back. In fact, once I'd been putting money aside to pay for a bank support worker to cover the normal DP worker's holiday pay. I got a bank statement and noticed that the money I'd saved had suddenly been withdrawn from my account. I checked with the bank and found the LA had gone into my account, checked the balance and without any warning, took back the £260 that I had saved to pay a reverse worker. I had to take the week off work as I didn't have the funds left to pay for cover.

Anyway – payroll companies. I also found out from my local ones that as well as charging for doing the payroll, all they did was to calculate the tax and national insurance and then notify me of their calculations so that I could pay the workers and complete all the necessary paperwork. That didn't feel like much of a service to me – I may resent it but I can work those figures out for myself. In a way, that's the easy bit – it's the paperwork that is so laborious.

Sorry – whinge over. I love the way that direct payments are sold to parents/carers as offering "choice and flexibility" but actually you can't really chose not to have them as then you are left with nothing. And then, having been forced to make a Hobson's choice, you get lumbered with having to do tax returns and LA account submissions.

I don't want to be an employer; I just want to be a Dad.

A Delightful Log

January 31, 2013

Here's a sentence that I never expected to write – I love Steven's daily reporting log. Note the singular "log", not "logs". Since that liberating meeting last September when we managed to extricate ourselves from those awful arse covering, tick box forms we had to complete for social services, we have just had one A4 book. There is no set format to it; it's more like a diary than a log, so it allows the support staff to express themselves in their own individual way. And that's what is so brilliant about it – the log perfectly reflects the unique relationships that Steven has with each of the workers. None of that nonsense like we had with the speech and language therapist who instructed us all to never use more than four words in a sentence with Steven and to stretch each vowel out like a piece of plasticine. It could never work. How do you answer the question: "Dad, what was Take That's 10th song called?". Answer – "It was Take That and LoooooooLooooooo singing Relight My Fire, Steve". It doesn't fit. And we're not robots.

The main reason for keeping a log at all is to have a record to produce to the CQC upon inspection. And I would hope that the CQC would find the record interesting and admire the ability of the staff to form meaningful, individual relationships with Steven. The staff read the log at the start of their shift but we tend to rely on verbal communication during a handover. I know that I get told the important news by the workers or Steven, so I read the log for entertainment.

We have five support workers in the team; five very different men, each with their own way of relating. I am very fond of all of them and know that Steven's life would be less fulfilling if they weren't around. I've shown them this blog post and they know it is written with deep affection. For this post, I'll call them Gary, Mark, Jason, Howard and Robbie.

Gary is Steven's longest serving support worker and still carries some of the scars of trying to support Steven during his year at the positive behaviour unit. He still gets anxious about his work being scrutinised unfavourably, even though I think he is great. His entries in the log go into minute detail, almost bordering on the pedantic: "At 7.53am, Steven had a moment of anxiety and thumped the arm of the sofa". "At 7.57am, he was calmer and ate a pear". He writes pages and pages and the reader tends to give up halfway through but I love the attention to detail.

Mark has a lot of experience working in care homes and writes formally, focusing almost solely on behaviour: "Steven interacted positively with other service users at the pool". It's interesting because this isn't how he interacts with Steven; they have great laughs together and he's very chilled but I guess he's used to that institutionalised way of writing.

Jason is a man of few words and so are his log entries. If you get more than three sentences from him, he's being verbose. He is the strong silent member of the team who Steven tends to rely on for help with tasks. His logs reflect this: "Changed sheets. Did washing. Cut Steven's hair".

Howard is newer and has bonded well with Steven over music. Subsequently all his log entries have a musical reference in them: "Steven enjoyed his time in the steam room where we sang Adam Ant songs"; "We played an M People CD whilst making cheese on toast".

Robbie is great and writes in rather exaggerated, almost theatrical language: "Steven had a delightful time at the Mencap Pool". "His mood was jolly as he chatted with his friends". I could read this stuff all day; it's like our life is chronicled by Enid Blyton.

Aren't they great. And what we sometimes do is read them back to Steven and he gets dead excited by hearing the narrative of his day. We could never have done that with the old START recording forms.

Never Forget: Howard Leaves Our Support Team

February 11, 2013

Calamity. No sooner had I pressed "enter" and published last week's post, "A Delightful Log", than Howard handed in his resignation with immediate effect. He had been on long term leave and decided not to come back. Howard was the worker who had created a great bond with Steven over their love of music. He would sing "Splish Splash" whilst doing bathtimes.

Never mind. Onwards and upwards as they say. We've had a reserve member of the team for a couple of months now, who filled in whilst Howard was on his holiday. So he has automatically been given Howard's shifts. What shall we call him? Ummmm …..Howard?

New Howard already has stamped his own mark on the daily log writing. He's got a rather odd way of writing that reads like he's hedging his bets: "Steven seemed calm"; "Steven appeared to enjoy himself at the gym". Nothing categorical; more like an uncertain perception. It reminds me of that wonderful speech of Inspector Morse in Masonic Mysteries when Lewis suggests that Morse may be being targeted by an old enemy: "SEEMS! There's no 'seem' about it Lewis. The minute we start seeming, we're really up shit creek". It's no big deal though; it's another style of logging that I find quite endearing and new Howard seems to be developing a good relationship with Steven.

I can't complain though. New Howard is a bit of a handyman and, without me asking, in the last four weeks has mended the broken living room door frame; regrouted the bath tiles; fixed the cupboard door in Steven's bedroom and sorted out my wobbly coffee table. All during the times when he's on a break between shifts. What a good bloke.

I'll sign off for now. Gary Barlow's got a dentist appointment, so I need to cover the last half of his shift.

Riding My High Horse

Every now and again, a story emerges from inside the social care world that presses all my buttons. I am political but I didn't intend the blog to be a political piece. Sometimes, you just have to get stuff off your chest:

- The New Deadly Sins: Resistance & Compliance
- He Who Pays The Advocate, Plays The.......
- When I'm Dead And Gone
- What Colour Is Your Medal?
- And The Winner Is ..... Not The Learning Disabled That's For Sure
- The Red Tape Challenge (Or Cutting The Ties To Humanity)
- In Your Service
- A Narrow View Of Family
- Marriage Lines
- A Game Of Social Care Trumps
- In A State

The New Deadly Sins: Resistance & Compliance

May 10, 2012

On the 29th May this year, a community care conference is taking place, entitled "Working With Highly Resistant Parents". the sub-title to the event is: "Practical strategies to tackle obstructive behaviour and disguised compliance". For more details of the event, see here:http://epidm.edgesuite.net/RBI/socialcare/SCCON/2012/HTML/SCCON_HRP_20120504.html

My apologies if it's difficult to think straight after reading that but your thought process is probably being drowned out by an orchestra of alarm bells.

Before we go into any observations, let me just point out a few items included in the programme for this day. At 11.45, a child protection consultant will deliver a lecture on: "Identifying indicators of disguised compliance". As a tasty appetizer before the lunch, the presentation includes, "How some parents mislead workers through passive, covert manipulation". After lunch, the delegates will enter the "virtual world" to see how game technology can help practitioners "manage situations where parents or carers are resistant, obstructive, deceptive or un-cooperative". And the big finale examines "where un-cooperative or deceitful behaviour may be as a result of a parental mental health problem" and alarmingly, "Parental grooming of professionals".

Where has this language and ideas come from? What robust thesis is it based on? Is there a justifiable reason for such an adversarial position? Why are the parents and carers cast as the dangerous enemy?

Court judgement after court judgement, after court judgement, repeatedly take the position that in the vast majority of cases, the parent/carer are the experts on the client's needs. It is the parents/carers who are most likely to genuinely know what is in the client's best interests. And out of old-fashioned concepts like love and duty, it is the parents/ carers who are most likely to genuinely fight for their children's best interests. Sadly, even the most committed professional with the upmost integrity cannot always do this as there will be other agendas at play, like budget cuts (or this week's latest Cameron word – "efficiencies"), political decisions or ignorance of the law etc.

The often quoted judgement of Justice Munby in Re:S, sums it up for me perfectly:

"[115] I am not saying that there is in law any presumption that mentally incapacitated adults are better off with their families: often they will be; sometimes they will not be. But respect for our human condition, regard for the realities of our society and the common sense to which Lord Oliver of Aylmerton referred in <u>In re KD</u>

..., surely indicate that the starting point should be the normal assumption that mentally incapacitated adults will be better off if they live with a family rather than in an institution – however benign and enlightened the institution may be, and however well integrated into the community – and that mentally incapacitated adults who have been looked after within their family will be better off if they continue to be looked after within the family rather than by the State.

[116] We have to be conscious of the limited ability of public authorities to improve on nature. We need to be careful not to embark upon 'social engineering'. And we should not lightly interfere with family life. If the State – typically, as here, in the guise of a local authority – is to say that it is the more appropriate person to look after a mentally incapacitated adult than her own partner or family, it assumes, as it seems to me, the burden – not the legal burden but the practical and evidential burden – of establishing that this is indeed so. And common sense surely indicates that the longer a vulnerable adult's partner, family or carer have looked after her without the State having perceived the need for its intervention, the more carefully must any proposals for intervention be scrutinised and the more cautious the court should be before accepting too readily the assertion that the State can do better than the partner, family or carer.

[117] At the end of the day, the simple point, surely, is this: the quality of public care must be at least as good as that from which the child or vulnerable adult has been rescued. Indeed that sets the requirement too low. If the State is to justify removing children from their parents or vulnerable adults from their relatives, partners, friends or carers it can only be on the basis that the State is going to provide a better quality of care than that which they have hitherto been receiving: see <u>Re F; F v Lambeth London Borough Council</u> [2002] 1 FLR 217, at para [43]."

However, despite a huge body of case-law supporting the above, rather than opening up a more collaborative way of working between parents and professionals, it seems to have driven the profession into a deeper bunker position, that quite frankly, can be frighteningly hostile. Umbrage is taken at the parents/carers view, and the idea of care goes for a burton as battle lines are drawn and weapons are employed. This is an arsenal of psychological weapons that can be terrifying for the parent/carer to face.

Of course the language and content at this conference exposes the massive divide between the professionals and the carers. The professional view seems to be that the position taken by parents/carers is because they have something untoward to hide; something dangerous and destructive to the client is being hidden. The carer's position, nine times out of ten, is that they are scared shitless about the enormous amount of power the professional holds. The carer is aware of countless stories of families being torn apart, by at best, ignorance, or at worst, unfortunately because of a vindictive, punitive individual or system. And if there is a difference of view between the carer and the professional, woe betides the carer if they chose to assert their view or challenge the alternative opinion. That is the reality for many many carers when complicated needs assessments are taking place and care plans are being drawn up. The carer has to be pretty sharp-witted to sift through the many agendas that are informing the process.

Let's examine some of the language of this conference: "Highly resistant parents" and "obstructive behaviour". In my counselling experience, people aren't resistant and obstructive for no reason. We resist something that doesn't feel right; something we feel isn't going to do us any good and may actually, cause us some harm. We may have smelled a rat and don't fancy entertaining that rat. We become obstructive when something we don't want or feel is no good for us, is being forced upon us. We feel backed into a corner. But the inference of this language is that the parent's behaviour is pathological; we are the rat that has been cornered. In my case, the council wanted to send my son to a hospital/care home 200 miles away, probably permanently. Was I highly resistant to this plan? YES. Was my behaviour obstructive? Probably, from the professional's perspective, by going to court and going public, I was obstructing their plan. Did I have any other choice? Well, that leads us on to the next succulent course on the conferences' menu: "Disguised Compliance".

I'm not entirely sure what that phrase means but I'm guessing that it means to pretend to be compliant, whilst behind the scenes, being anything but compliant. This is the professionals' equivalent of wanting their cake and eating it. Even when it goes against your better judgement, we cannot be resistant and obstructive; we cannot fake compliance. We have to be wholeheartedly compliant, with no reservations or misgivings. The professional always knows best, and my God, have we got to be grateful for that. I've written many times that I regularly attended meetings where there were 8 professionals present and me. It was very intimidating. Nearly all of the plans proposed at these meetings, I was uneasy with. But, I learned to choose my battles, so with some of the less life threatening plans, I probably fell into "disguised compliance". And then went straight home and phoned the solicitor. Or Private Eye. All fuelled by nothing other than desperation on my part to avert a catastrophe but galling for the professionals because I wasn't playing ball, although it may have looked like I was in the team.

I love the quote from Judge Endersligh in the judgement A London Authority V JH. In this case, the LA were furious that the man wanted to care for his wife at home and not be placed in a care home. They got round the wife's views by classifying her as lacking mental capacity. One of the professional's weapons at the hearing was the assertion of the husband's "repeated un-cooperation". Fortunately the judge had their number and gave them very short shrift:

"On many occasions (in the local authority statements and submissions, and in court) it has been asserted by the local authority that Mr H is unable to compromise or to reach a reasonable compromise and, by implication, that trying further to enlist his support and co-operation would be a fruitless exercise.

Mr H is a devoted husband, and I think a proud man, who finds it difficult to accept anything but the best for his wife, and this forms part of the picture.

However, I also find that Mr H has compromised his position since these proceedings begun in various important ways. He has compromised on the number of carer hours he seeks; he has agreed to occupational therapy and carer's assessments; he has agreed to proposals for GP, District Nurse, community matron visits; he has agreed to abide by a review of Mrs H's Linkline needs; he has put forward a constructive proposal in relation to the deployment of carers.

It is not only Mr H who at times has been unwilling to compromise a strongly-held opinion about the care and treatment which Mrs H must receive in her best interests. Since the start of these proceedings the local authority has not compromised any of its demands.

When significant issues have been raised in court, time and again the local authority has told me that Mr H is not willing to compromise, rather than that neither of us will compromise. Of course, what they mean is that he is not willing to concede the relevant point and neither are they. Compromise, as opposed to concession or surrender, is an agreement that involves both parties giving up part of their preferred position in order to reach a working agreement.

In his statement of 5 May 2011, the social worker Mr C says that the respite issue "has proved to be a long standing stumbling block that Mr H has always consistently felt unable to compromise on."

The way that sentence is phrased is illuminating. Mr C does not say "which the parties have felt unable to compromise" or "which the local authority has felt unable to compromise on." Here, the local authority did not offer any increase of respite hours. They were not asking Mr H to compromise but to concede. In short, they were not willing to compromise their position."

What happened to the idea of public service? In the not too distant past, the idea was that the professionals were meant to serve us; they were meant to cooperate with us – the customers. It's a shame but in the social care world that idea has been flipped on its head to such an extent that the idea of service is now laughable. It is never about the service user or the carers anymore – their needs come secondary (if at all) to the needs of the service. Do you read the agenda for the conference and get any sense that the end result, the driving force is about service? My sense was it was all about self-serving; fuelling a distrustful state that has completely lost sight of its basic function. Justice Peter Jackson made the following statement about the role of the state in Neary Vs Hillingdon:

"Nonetheless, two central principles are clear.

21. The first is that it is undoubtedly lawful for actions to be taken by families and local authorities, acting together on the basis of a careful assessment of the best interests of incapacitated persons. The vast majority of arrangements are made in this way and involve no breach of the rights of the persons concerned. Where there is a deprivation of liberty (referred to as a "DOL") a specific statutory code exists to provide safeguards.

22. The second central principle concerns cases of disagreement. The ordinary powers of a local authority are limited to investigating, providing support services, and where appropriate referring the matter to the court. If a local authority seeks to regulate, control, compel, restrain, confine or coerce it must, except in an emergency, point to specific statutory authority for what it is doing or else obtain the appropriate sanction of the court: again see <u>Re A and C</u> (above) and the authorities referred to therein".

The finale is the really scary part. I have this awful picture of the audience being whipped into a frenzy by this juncture and the icing on the cake is to diagnose the parent/carer as mentally ill, or that they are engaged in grooming. Lets up the ante at the final knockings with two of the, still, biggest taboos in our society. A mental health diagnosis in the hands of a non mental health clinician leads us into very murky waters indeed. All sorts of plans can be railroaded through if we can show that the carer isn't mentally capable of caring, or of making an informed decision about the person they care for. Mental Health = Risk, so therefore the professional with their craving for risk management plans will be galvanised into action and the carer is put firmly in their mentally ill or incapable place.

Grooming is quite a disgusting insinuation. These days, that word is used solely in connection with paedophilia and involves the psychological and physical intrusion of an innocent, vulnerable party. Now, that concept is being used by casting the carer as the groomer and the professional as the innocent child. I don't believe that idea stands up to any scrutiny whatsoever but the scare mongering language will chill the blood of anyone presented with that accusation. And the inference is obvious: if the parent can groom an adult professional, just think what they are doing to the person they are caring for. these are the heavy weapons of the war but to quote Basil Fawlty: "Who started the war?".

I work on the basic operating principle that if what I am being presented with feels totally at odds with my experience of the situation, then probably, the opposite of what is being presented is true. To that end, I'd like to propose an alternative conference on 29th May, called "Working With Highly Resistant Professionals". Is anyone compliant with this idea?

He Who Pays The Advocate, Calls The …….

August 3, 2012

Yesterday, there was an intriguing comment left on my blog from a man who lives in the same borough as me. Basically, back in June, he wanted to book a place on the annual local carer's conference, organised and run by our local authority. He contacted the LA to arrange a place but was told that the bookings must be done through our local carers' organisation. He did this but was told however, that as he is not a member of the carers' organisation, he was not entitled to a place.

Whys has this stirred me into writing? I belong to several carers groups and forums and one theme that has cropped up with depressing regularity over the past couple of years is how the many large and local carers and disabled organisations that exist, seem to have become increasingly detached from serving the needs of the people they were set up to represent – the carers and the disabled.

If you look at any of the large organisation's websites, you will see them declare advocacy and support as two of their main services. So, why does it feel that these organisations have become more remote when the need for their advocacy input has never been greater.

When I was in the midst of my battle in 2010, I approached all the major organisations for help: the NAS, Mencap, Carers UK etc. I also contacted all my local ones as well. None of them were able to offer any help. In fact, it was the local organisations that felt the most cold towards my desperate pleas for help. Funnily enough, once the final judgement had been handed down, all the national organisations made a statement about the case, along the lines of how awful it had been that such a thing could happen; how difficult it had been for me to find support and what a landmark moment this was for disabled people. Perhaps that's what their role is now: to proclaim rather than to provide.

I remember walking past my local carer's office last year and seeing a huge poster in the window, celebrating its partnership with the Local Authority. I felt uneasy. I'm not saying for one moment that the authorities and the local groups shouldn't work together – that would be completely counterproductive. But I do question whether a client can receive truly independent advocacy when these organisations have such close relationships.

Lots of local authorities farm out some of their services to local organisations. A friend of mine has been involved in a ridiculous boomerang game because her LA has given over their carers' assessment service to the local carer's organisation. One does the assessment; the other holds the purse strings. Goodness knows what the problem is but eight months after having a "preliminary carer's assessment", no obvious outcome has been identified or acted upon. This same carers agency receives over 75% of its funding from the LA – a large proportion of that 75% coming from their annual carers grant, which I've always believed is meant to be for the carers. I'm pretty sure that's what central government intended when they allocate these funds to the LAs. So, if my friend wants to challenge this inactivity, where does she get her advocacy from? She won't be able to get it from the obvious place – the carers agency because they have become an intrinsic part of the process. Item two on this agency's mission statement is: "providing carers with support and advice to access their rights".

The government's white paper on social care makes hardly any mention of advocacy at all which is very worrying. But even if advocacy had been more prominently on the agenda, who is going to provide it from a totally neutral position. Challenging authority is a lonely, frightening business. It's made worse if you walk through the doors of a place purporting to support you, only to find they are indirectly or directly, part of the authority too. It doesn't do much for your feelings of hope.

In a Panglossian world, every vulnerable person should be offered an advocate – an independent one who could really act in their best interests without a fettered agenda. Not every offer would be taken up, which is fair enough, but for those that did, the world might seem less lonely or frightening.

If there was the choice between central government issuing grants to LAs who in turn issue grants to local agencies to support the disabled and their carers; or central government issuing grants directly to advocacy services to provide support, I know which one I would choose.

When I'm Dead And Gone

August 8, 2012

Yesterday was my day off from work. I had big plans: housework first thing; then off to an early showing of the new Batman and then home to do a new tape with Steven. (We're working through the alphabet at the moment and yesterday were up to "J", so anticipating The Jam, Just Jack, Johnny Cash amongst others). The carpets remain unhoovered, Tom Hardy missed my presence in Studio 2, but John and Edward got an airing. Instead, I found myself sitting in front of my computer screen, paralysed by the Serious Case Review report into Winterbourne View (see here: http://hosted.southglos.gov.uk/wv/report.pdf) I swung between sobbing and barely controllable rage. I had to have four attempts before I could finish it as I found it so emotionally draining. A serious thumbs up to the author, Dr Margaret Flynn, who didn't pull any punches at all.

There have been several commentaries on the report, written much more eloquently than I could. My overriding feeling is what total cunts they all were. Not just the 11 perpetrators of such vile abuse, but all the other cast of characters in this terrible drama. I found myself getting just as angry by the quote from an anonymous Castlebeck director as I did about the violence his (or her) staff carried out. How about this statement for brass neck: 'We've learned our lessons and the review marks the start of a new chapter for care in our sector.' That's alright then. Now fuck off and go back to counting your profits. What sort of spun out society have we become that people believe that kind of statement is okay? On several occasions throughout the report, the author mentions Castleback's lack of co-operation with the review, falling back on that old chestnut; the information is commercially sensitive. So, commercial sensitivity comes way ahead of the sensitivities of the patients and their families. It's good we all know where we stand.

What can we say about the South Gloucstershire safeguarding adults team? Not a lot. Except, you've got your priorities all wrong and if you spent a little less time arse covering and more time looking after your clients, perhaps…… It galls me but doesn't surprise me that the only time they really sprung into action is when there were complaints made about patients or their families. Those complaints about patients or families were always acted upon but complaints about the staff etc just hit an arse covered wall and died. I've learned over the last few years dealing with adult social care that there always has to be a human shield, and invariably that shield is either the lowest ranks or the situation gets completely flipped over so that the aggrieved becomes the aggressor. When Steven was attending the Day Centre back in 2008, he was assaulted by one of the staff there; he was kicked three times on the leg and had a cup of hot coffee poured over him. The attacker who was quite senior and the shift leader tried to cover it up. It took two junior members of staff to report it and persisted to such an extent that it couldn't be ignored. We weren't informed of the attack until 8 hours after it happened; even then the social worker presented it to us anonymously, so I (to my shame) assumed it was another service user that launched the attack. The two junior members of staff had a very hard time and a lot of pressure was applied to them to dilute the incident. Nevertheless, the senior staff and managers could use the attacker and the shift leader as their shield. In 2010, when Steven was at the positive behaviour unit, I insisted that Steven's normal support workers continued working with him. But in the authority's eyes, they were lower than the unit's own staff, so they became the new shield – if anything untoward happened, they carried the can. Two of Steven's workers were suspended over an incident where they were put into a terrible situation by the unit's shift leader. A week later, two unit staff had a massive argument in front of Steven and one threw a heavy object at the other, smashing a window. Nothing happened to either of them. All of the managers and social work staff involved in the year of Steven's illegal detainment are still there in the same posts; there were no consequences for them at all.

Now comes the really hard bit to write. It's not a new thought, prompted by the events at Winterbourne; I've had sleepless nights for several years over the issue. What happens to Steven when I'm dead and gone. Every time I go to a meeting with social services, at some point during the meeting, I am asked the same question: "What are your plans for Steven for the future?" I've probably given the same answer over 40 times now but it doesn't stop me being asked again. Perhaps, I haven't given the right answer but they don't want to tell me that? Perhaps, it's just a box to be ticked and my answer is completely irrelevant because they already know the answer in Steven's case? Who knows? For what it's worth, I'd like (and Steven would too) for Steven to have his own place with live in support. He finds mixing with his peers very challenging, so for me, a multi occupied place would be out of the question. Steven could either continue to live in our privately rented property (landlady has already acknowledged that would be okay) or at some point, Steven would have the home we own that his mother currently lives in.

But deep down, I know that if I drop dead tomorrow, none of that will happen. I know that by the time I'm being laid out at the undertakers, Steven will be in a car to that care home/hospital in Wales that the council wanted to send him to in 2010. His links with everything he knows and loves will be terminated as quickly as my life had just ended. And wherever he ends up, he could find himself in a lovely, empathic place or he could find himself in another positive behaviour unit. Or another Winterbourne View.

And it's too painful to write any more on the subject

What Colour Is Your Medal?

September 10, 2012

The Paralympics have been incredible. Two weeks of inspirational performances that have been an absolute joy to watch. We now have a new roll call of sporting heroes, who happen to be disabled.

And today, we have seen some new phrases doing the rounds: "The 2012 Legacy"; "The Bright New Dawn For The Disabled"; "Barriers Have Been Broken"; "An Enlightened World". Anthemic and motivating language. And all in capital letters.

My only unease of the past fortnight has been trying to square what I have been watching on TV with my day-to-day experience of caring for a disabled adult and being part of the disabled world. I'm sure like a lot of parents and carers over the two weeks; I've had the fleeting thought: "Shall I sign Steven up for some javelin sessions?" But it is a fleeting thought.

So, will there be a bright new dawn for the young man in the wheelchair, I see regularly, being pushed round the precinct for the fourth time this week by the dis-interested support worker? What will the legacy be for my friend's daughter who is now confined to her home six days a week because her day centre has been closed down? Will my other single parent friend who gets three hours a fortnight respite from her 24/7 caring be able to break down some new barriers? And when I go to my next meeting with social services to discuss indicative budgets and behaviour management plans, will I be stepping into a new enlightened world? I hope so, because these things are just as important as the wonderful David Weir's medal haul.

This week I will be hard pressed to take Steven for his shot putt training. Tomorrow, I have to meet the social worker for a FACE assessment. The present care package is working very well but I fear that after we've been fed into a RAS, I may not be able to afford the archery coaching. On Wednesday I have to attend the Housing Benefit appeal meeting, just to try to preserve a roof over out heads. Come Friday, I will be taking Steven for his six monthly blood test to make sure that his medication isn't fucking up his organs. And I've still got to try to fit in a mental capacity assessment with the GP to ascertain whether he has the capacity to manage his own finances. Until the test is done, he cannot receive the damages he was awarded back in July. I was reading Ellie Simmonds' weekly training diary yesterday; her week feels very different to mine.

Yesterday did have an inspirational moment. The previous Sunday, our local Mencap Pool reopened after its summer break. The couple who run the pool had gone away for the weekend to visit friends, who incidentally we met when we went to Yarmouth in July. When Steven saw the couple yesterday, he went up and said: "Did you enjoy your holiday in Yarmouth, Jean?" Now, that's quite an awesome moment. It's pretty rare for Steven to start up a conversation with an enquiry about the other person's well-being.

For Steven, it was quite possibly a gold medal moment.

And The Winner Is........Not The Learning Disabled, That's For Sure

October 28, 2012

This week saw the sentencing of the 11 workers involved in the horrific abuse at Winterbourne View. The sentences ranged from two years to community service; derisory sentences for horrible crimes. And sadly, it shows once again that the learning disabled draw a very short straw when it comes to access to justice.

What of Castlebeck, the owners of Winterbourne View? Well, not a lot actually. After the sentencing of their staff, the company issued the following statement:

"Castlebeck welcomes the finalisation of the legal process concerning the wholly unacceptable and criminal behaviour witnessed at Winterbourne View.

When those events at Winterbourne View Independent Hospital were exposed in May 2011, the board and the company's then Chief Executive expressed their unequivocal and unreserved regret to the service users involved and their families.

They also gave a clear commitment to protect the safety and well-being of all those who use Castlebeck's services and swift and decisive action was taken as soon as the allegations were raised almost 18 months ago".

Which I think, roughly translated means: "Ha ha ha. Phew, got out of that one. Now fuck off, we've got profits to count".

These sort of statements are so much part of our culture now, that they have become meaningless. They are written by committee and I don't think either the author or the reader/listener understands or believes a word of them.

If that statement doesn't stick in the throat, what follows causes a severe nauseous attack. It was announced this week that Castlebeck are sponsoring an award at this year's Royal College of Nursing awards. And not just any old award – they are sponsoring the learning disability nurse of the year award. I swear to God, when I read that, I thought I'd stumbled across an episode of The Thick of It. Brass neck doesn't even come close.

I think the point of this is that the management in these sort of scandals nearly always come out of it relatively unscathed. I've written about it before, but from June 2008 until September 2008, Steven was attending a unit on a day basis (This was one of those many occasions that the council suddenly stopped his support package without warning, so he had no choice but to go to this place). One day, he was assaulted by one the workers there; he was kicked at least three times and had a cup of coffee poured over him. The council launched their own investigation (whitewash) but the CPS prosecuted on Steven's behalf. The worker was found guilty, although I never found out what his sentence was. The shift leader, who tried to cover the incident up was sacked. However, a couple of months after the incident, the manager of the unit was promoted to a senior position within the civic centre and the assistant manager was promoted to manager. All done and dusted. And of course, not a single person lost their job or suffered any consequences for the illegal actions of 2010.

Whilst on the subject of that unit, I read their latest CQC report this week. The first thing that struck me was that, sometime during the last year, the unit has changed from an assessment and treatment centre with a stay there between 3 to 18 months, to a generic care home. How did that happen? Is it not a positive behaviour unit anymore? The council's own website still says that it is. And what flimsy document the report is. The unit was found to be compliant in all areas but it looks like only one service user was asked for feedback and only one family member. The rest of the feedback came from staff at the unit and other interested professionals. There are some good things that happen at the unit and there are some very good, dedicated staff there but I didn't recognise the place from the report. Do people actually make a decision on where to place their loved ones on the basis of a CQC report? I hope not.

So, that was the week that was. The residents of Winterbourne View and their families will get on with healing the scars of their awful experience; the 11 staff will get on with the business of prison/community service life. And the Castlebeck managers will be dusting off their tuxedos in preparation for a gala awards ceremony.

The Red Tape Challenge (Or Cutting The Ties to Humanity)

November 8, 2012

This week, the department of Health began its consultation process for its "Red Tape Challenge" in health and social care. You can read about it here (http://www.dh.gov.uk/health/2012/11/red-tape-challenge/). As it is legally bound to do, the DofH is consulting; inviting comments from interested parties on the areas that it has identified as "red tape". It's a clever, nasty move couching the proposed cuts in those terms – who in the right mind would argue against cutting bureaucratic red tape.

But as they say, the devil is the detail (and there's plenty of devilment in this document). And by heck, there is a lot of detail to get through in the paper, much of it over my head. One area that hits me on the head obviously is the Deprivation of Liberty safeguards; a clunky, flawed piece of legislation but until a better alternative is in place, the only means a vulnerable person has of challenging being unlawfully deprived of their liberty by the authorities. Safeguards are lifelines – not pesky red tape.

Two crucial aspects of the safeguards are to enable the person deprived of their liberty to have a relevant person's representative (RPR), who is usually a family member or carer. Who can help the voice of the detained person be heard and challenge the DoL if it's against their wishes. Secondly, the person is entitled to an Independent Mental capacity Advocate (IMCA) who can provide professional backing to the detained person. Without these two interventions, the vulnerable person is quite alone and completely reliant on the supervisory body acting in their best interests and getting it right without any other concealed agenda. And as we know, they do sometimes get it terribly wrong. The Department of Health has decided that the RPR and the IMCA roles are red tape and can be cut out. No professional advocacy. No nuisance relative challenging the professional view. No access to justice if an injustice has occurred.

To personalise for a moment, without my voice and eventually the voice of the IMCA, Steven would have ended up in a care home over 200 miles from his home ("facing a life in public care that he does not want or does not need"). He would have been left to rot there, losing contact with family and friends and all the things that are important to him and make his quality of life. His detainment was an illegal one based on flawed best interests assessments and duplicitous actions from the LA. But none of that matters to the DoH because it is just red tape and has to be cut away.

When I started writing this blog, I had the idea of throwing everything into it; a mish mash of stuff that interested me. Over the months though, it seems to have become about two things: understanding the fake language that underpins most of our "care" discourse and exposing the hidden agendas behind the spin. I realise that is a grandiose statement but I do really believe it is the biggest challenge of the day. I work as a counsellor and I hear on a daily basis how much our psychological well-being is damaged by this hellish nonsense; how much our sense of our reality is skewed by the outward presentation.

So it is more than likely that behind the spin of the Red Tape Challenge is our two old friends: money and power. The money one is obvious; on a basic level IMCA's cost money but they are only the starting point. Think of the efficiency savings that can be made on the legal aid bill (which the detained person is automatically entitled to by the way). But RPRs don't cost a single penny, although like the IMCA. they can trigger off the costly court process. Where I live, there are at least 24 very senior managers within the social care hierarchy but who is going to suggest that there might be a bit of red tape there that could be cut.

No RPR. No IMCA. The committed professionals within the field who might want to challenge the challenge but are buggared because they are in the system. What chance does the vulnerable person have with all those people out of the picture.

We must fight this. Families, legal professionals, social care workers must come together and make sure that the precious few human rights that a vulnerable person has aren't savaged any further.

This is a call to arms! Who's in?

In Your Service

December 29, 2012

What's with all the hostility from those in public service? It seems more and more to me that the starting position is usually a defensive one and it goes downhill from there. Trying to have a conversation with someone in authority these days reminds me of those moments when as a kid you are expecting to be caught out by your parent ("Can you come in the living room a minute Mark?" – "I haven't done anything Mum").

Every statement I read from the DWP is un-necessarily aggressive. Their statements usually appear at the end of some report where the DWP official figures or statistics have been revealed to be dodgy or downright lies. The DWP response is often quite wordy but might just as well say "Fuck off – who the hell do you think you are".

Today I got a letter from the Tax office informing me that I may have not sent my self assessment back in April. That is the opening sentence and the use of the word "may" suggests a pleasant discussion may next take place. No siree. From that point on, the letter is a succession of threats. Threats of penalties that gets increasingly severe. I'm surprised the letter doesn't end with the threat of castration. For the record, I submitted my tax return on 8th April with a covering letter and thankfully sent it by recorded delivery because Mr Paranoid thinks this might be a new way for HMRC to make a bit of money – tell people they didn't submit a return and then give them a £10 per day penalty. But my point is, after the placid opening sentence, the attack is launched and there is never the possibility that perhaps the error may be at the official end.

This brings me to my fabulous conversation with the direct payments officer at Hillingdon the week before Christmas. The direct payments were due on 17th December. It's an important month; not only do the workers want their money for Christmas (not unreasonable) but the PAYE is due at the end of December and if the attitude in the above paragraph is anything to go by, I don't want to run the risk of incurring a fine. So, I checked the DP account on 17th – nothing there. Checked it again the following day – nothing there. I phoned the council and was promised a call back later that day after they looked into it. No call came, so I phoned again on 19th (after checking the account again). I waited 35 minutes to be put through and before I even got to end of my opening sentence was told, "I've checked. It has definitely been processed. There's nothing more I can do". End of conversation. I phoned the bank again just to see if the credit had disappeared into some sort of "pending ether" but to no avail. Five minutes later, the bank phoned me back. The very helpful woman had checked and the direct payments had been paid into my personal account (it hadn't occurred to me to look there!). I thought I'd better phone the direct payment team back to tell them:

Me: Guess what. I've found it.

DP: I've already told you it was processed on time.

Me: It was in my personal account.

DP: (suspicious) How did it get there? All transactions have to take place from the one account for the direct payment audit.

Me: How did it get there! I guess you sent it there.

DP: That couldn't happen.

Me: But you pay me. I don't have anything to do with it until it's in the account.

DP: We don't have access to your personal account. (That's not strictly true. They overpaid my housing benefit once and went straight into the account the next day and took it back).

Me: Don't worry about it. I've transferred it into the DP account now.

DP: You must have changed the bank details.

Me: Look. Have you got any record, Phone call, letter from me giving alternative bank details?

DP: I shall have to change it back straightaway. We can't have this happen again Mr Neary.

Me; Just a thought. I've just had a payment into my personal account from your homeless team to cover my housing benefit. Could the bank details have been altered by them?

DP: You gave my colleague in housing different bank details?

Me: Of course. The rent can't go into the DP account.

DP: Ah. See. That's where the misunderstanding occurred. Leave it with me Mr Neary – I'll get it sorted by next month's payment.

The inference during the whole conversation was that I done something wrong. Worse – something suspicious. Was I trying to pocket the direct payment? That's what it felt like. What obviously happened is that the council must have this one massive payment system and it can't handle different payments going into different accounts. Where's the shame in her saying: "Mr Neary, the truth is, we've got a computer system that dates back to the time that Showwaddywaddy were having hit records. You may have to start playing pass the parcel every month and transfer the payments from one account to another. And next time you're in Greggs – have a cream cake on me for the inconvenience".

When did this change in attitude happen? Someone, somewhere must have decided that it was a good policy to adopt with members of public; people using the service. Now it seems to me pretty endemic.

A Narrow View of "Family"

January 5, 2013

Hillingdon Council sent me a lovely happy new year present the other day – their submission to the Social Security First Tier Tribunal. Hopefully, not setting the tone for my 2013, it comprised 80 odd pages, that took ages to read through and absorb.

I'm not going to go into detail again about why they cancelled my housing benefit as I've blogged about it elsewhere but basically they decided after four years of awarding it to me, that a month after Steven's damages were awarded by the court, they needed to review my claim and came to the decision that the house where my wife lives should be taken into account as capital available to me. Nothing has changed since July 2009 when Hillingdon told me that if I didn't move out of the marital home, they would issue a safeguarding alert on Steven as his mother's mental health state was having an adverse effect on him and the sustainability of the care package. Included in the council's own evidence bundle is a letter from the social worker at the time ("There's always something or other……") supporting the move. Nothing has changed between August 2009 and November 2012, except the way Hillingdon are viewing the second property issue.

One thing that has struck me reading their submission is how out of touch the benefits regulations are with the real experiences of the adult learning disabled and their families. As well as the obvious legal argument that my solicitor has submitted (basically that they have misinterpreted or misdirected themselves), we have also made submissions under the Equalities Act. In my case, there are three people involved in the story: me, my autistic adult son (who lives with me) and my incapacitated wife (who lives in the old marital home).

The HB regulations say that a second property can be disregarded if "it is occupied by an incapacitated partner or incapacitated relative of Mr Neary". They argue my wife is not my "partner" as we live apart and she is not a relative because a wife/husband/spouse is not included in the list of "defined relatives". My sister's partner counts as a relative, so does an uncle but not a marital partner. Strange!

Next step, the HB regulations state the second property can be disregarded if "it is occupied by an incapacitated relative of a member of Mr Neary's family.

So, my wife is a relative of my son but Steven doesn't count as a member of my family (He would have counted in the previous list alongside uncles and sister's partners!). And the only criteria for discounting him as a member of my family is that he is financially independent of me. That is of course true but to differing degrees in every other aspect of his life, he is dependent on me. And will be as long as I continue to be his carer. That seems quite discriminatory to me – no acknowledgement of the special circumstances of a learning disabled adult living in the family home.

If any legal people are reading this, is there a possible CRPD issue going on here?

So, that's that. At least 14 weeks to wait before the appeal is heard and little chance of success if the judge sticks to these very narrow definitions and views of "family".

Marriage Lines

February 9, 2013

It's been a funny old week for marriage. We've had the fabulous equal marriage vote in the Commons (and if it starts the implosion of the Tories, all the better). But apart from that, I've been thinking of the very narrow thinking of the State about marriage. Three different stories have made me think:

First off is the stories that have been emerging about the hateful bedroom tax. ITV News have been running a series of articles about how people will be affected and this particular story I found particularly harrowing:

http://www.itv.com/news/update/2013-02-01/couple-break-down-over-prospect-of-bedroom-tax/

As the woman has cerebral palsy, she tends to move around a lot in the night and has spasms, so her obviously devoted husband and carer sleeps in the 2nd bedroom most nights. However, the simplistic bedroom tax rules sees a married couple and rules that they are only allowed one bedroom; they will be charged for the second one that the husband sleeps in. I have it on good authority that the Queen and Prince Phillip have separate beds but then I don't suppose the bedroom tax applies to them. Basic rule 1: married couple = 1 bed in 1 bedroom. End of.

Second story is my own. I've written at length about my housing benefit situation that is now going to appeal. It all hinges on the very narrow definition of "wife" and "family". Although I still care deeply for my wife and we are only apart because it is in Steven's best interests to be apart, we are no longer considered husband and wife because we live apart. Similarly, Steven is not counted as a member of my family as he is over 18 and seen as independent. Obviously he is financially dependent but that is where his dependence ends. BUt the whole of the council's case is built on the fact that my wife is no longer my wife and my son is not a member of my family.

The final story is the latest Court of Protection judgement concerning a man with serious brain damage and the question of whether he has the mental capacity to marry.

http://www.bailii.org/ew/cases/EWHC/COP/2012/B29.html

The judge decided that the man, AK, did not have the capacity to understand the full implications of marriage and annulled the man's marriage. In a sense, the judge couldn't decide anything else and there were several pieces of evidence that led him to make the judgement he did. However, it made me think of two things: Firstly, there is little reference to best interests in the judgement (I acknowledge that wasn't the remit of the case) and the consequence of the judgement is that AK will now be living alone in a care unit, rather than in the home he was sharing with his wife, who despite some of the things she did, obviously loves and cares for him. There may have been huge problems ahead for them as a couple but what he's left with is a life in a loveless care home. Secondly, I thought that once again for me, this is a case where the hoops a learning disabled person has to go through to live a life are hugely greater than the non disabled person. How many married readers of this blog had to demonstrate they understood the concept of marriage and the implications of the married state before they tied the knot? When I got married at 23, I was as green as grass. I knew I was marrying someone I loved, perhaps we would have kids one day, live in a nice house and in our retirement, listen to Just A Minute together and wear matching cardigans. In my work as a counsellor, I see people daily who are in bad marriages (their term) and if I had a pound for every time someone has said "If I knew then what I know now….", I'd probably have, oh, about £875.75. It feels to me that once again, where some leeway should be afforded the learning disabled around their decision making capacity, in reality for them, the bar is set higher than the non learning disabled.

And I am old enough to remember Richard Briers and Prunella Scales in Marriage Lines.

A Game of Social Care Trumps

March 9, 2013

Here's a question for you. Is there any area within the social care field where money isn't the trump card? Is there any argument that can be put forward that isn't going to be trumped by money?

I've been thinking a lot about trumping recently (I must sort out my appalling flatulence). In the ongoing saga of our probable homelessness, Hillingdon's argument is that their housing allocation policy of non eligibility to social housing for anyone with capital over £30,000 trumps their duty of care towards a vulnerable person. Forget the moral dimension of the situation; Steven only has the capital because of the illegal act in 2010. A LOCAL policy takes precedent over the threat of an extremely vulnerable adult becoming homeless. It also trumps a High Court best interest's judgement as well. There aren't many people I'd guess who would consider it in Steven's best interests to be forced to become a private tenant and have to use all of his damages award to pay his rent. Trumped by money. Trumped by local policy. Fuck the ethical element and the human being at the core of its game.

I was able to use the money trump myself once. Hillingdon's reluctance to provide any respite for Steven except at the unit where he was unlawfully held for a year, was couched in terms like "encouraging independence", "flexibility" etc. They also brought into the debate "an equitable service for all service users" and woes betide you if you try to challenge that with a person centered argument. Anyway, after weeks of pointless negotiation because we weren't allowed to discuss the real agenda (money), I managed to get the support workers to agree to do overnight home respite for a ridiculously small fee in comparison to the figures we weren't talking about. I submitted a proposal and we never talked about independence, flexibility or equitability again. Money talks.

For the past 18 months, I have been following the sad local story about Hillingdon's plan to close its three day centres and replace them with one smaller hub. (The word "hub" should immediately be a money alert sign). Everyone knows that what it really is all about is money and in all probability, in a year's time, some impressive looking blocks of flats will appear in the place where the day centres used to be. A hardy group of parent carers challenged the plan and just before it was about to come before the court, the council backtracked and said they would extend the consultation period. A few months on, the consultation period is over and the three day centres will soon be rubble. For some strange reason, I get sent the minutes of the monthly meetings between the parent carer group and the council managers. It's absorbing reading; it's like a 2013 version of The Kings New Clothes. The council's line, of course, is that the new arrangements at the hub will increase the service user's independence and the accompanying personal budget will empower them choice and flexibility wise. It doesn't hold up to any scrutiny whatsoever. One service user spent her time at her day centre preparing her meals for the evening, whilst at the same time enjoying the friendships she has built there. Sounds pretty cool to me. Now, she'll spend the same time window shopping in Argos. And by the time she has paid for the support worker's wages and their lunch out of her personal budget, she won't have anything left to actually go into Argos and buy something. But then again, that's the beauty of personal budgets. So the meeting goes into incredible detail about peripheral stuff and money never rears its formidable head. It's conjuring tricks at their finest. It's like discussing Martha & The Muffins' greatest hits without any reference to Echo Beach.

Steven has a bizarre card game of Coronation Street trumps. We don't understand the rules but an Albert Tatlock trumps a Hayley Cropper. I've been embroiled in social care systems and their double speak for ages and I still haven't found my Albert Tatlock that can trump their money card. Especially when their money card is disguised as an independent, flexible Curly Watts.

The Minor Royal Who Becomes A Vampire

When you are 53rd in line to the throne, deep down you know that your chances of ascension are next to nothing. But throughout his 27 years, the thing that irked Anthony Hindenberg-Dink, 6th Earl of Newport Pagnelshire, the most, was the complete absence of any public interests in his vapid life. Unfortunately, he was saddled with an ego the size of a small Commonwealth country, so he refused to take this whitewash of his qualities, lying down. High jinx at Eton didn't garner a single column inch in the broadsheets, whilst his fellow members of the Bullingham Club went on to greater things. A succession of unsuitable sexual encounters passed the red tops by. Fuelled by a jaw dropping drug habit, Anthony allowed paranoia to enter this soul. He believed that some effing lackey at Buck House had authorised a news blackout on his sensational pastimes. Jesus Christ – even a thoroughly sordid weekend with Kerry Katona failed to arouse even the most salacious of Fleet Street's finest.

Bitter and twisted, Anthony took to spending meandering days and nights at his Club and it was there one evening in August that he met the shadowy figure, who only answered to the name of "Le Comte". For four short balmy weeks they became great friends – "Jolly decent chap the old comte – marvellously generous", was the fulsome reference Anthony offered to anyone stupid enough to listen. On the third week of their acquaintance, The Count, sensing that it was time to test the boundaries, introduced his eager protégé to the most invigorating of tomato based liquors. It had a warm, syrupy taste that was most palatable and left one licking for more. Surprisingly, they never led to any tippsi wippsiness but were very moorish.

And then, as suddenly as The Count had appeared in Anthony's life, he disappeared. There had been vague mutterings of having to attend to his Romanian business affairs but nothing concrete. Ah well, it was an interesting interlude whilst it lasted – a jolly decent chap to have in the old address book.

It was a week after The Count's vanishing act that Anthony grasped the full nature of their brief encounter. In the intervening week, Anthony had returned to the club and was bemused to discover that Jake, the maitre D, did not have the recipe for his favourite tomato based cocktail. Even more confusingly, Jake was insistent that he had never served The Count anything other than treble gins. Other strange things started to come to Anthony's notice: he was sleeping more during the day and had started to feel repulsed by, until then, the staple of his daily diet – garlic mushrooms. Anthony's mother had suffered terribly during her menopause, so perhaps this was an early, male version of the same.

It was the first Saturday in September and Anthony awoke at midday, slightly groggy, having discovered the delights of a heroin slammer the night before. He stumbled out of bed and immediately fell arse over tip. Or rather arse over Gustav. Lying on his bedroom floor was Gustav, his faithful basset hound. The poor animal was stone dead and on closer inspection, there could be no escaping the fact that his throat had been slit. In a state of abject horror, Anthony clutched his bedpost and caught sight of himself in his full length dressing mirror. His jimjams were covered in blood and his eiderdown was splattered with claret.

"Think man, think. Is there any connection between the state of your nightclothes and poor deceased Gustav?"

A fleeting idea, so horrendous flickered in Anthony's brain that he immediately blocked it out. But as summer turned to autumn, it became increasingly impossible to bury this new character development in the overstocked family vault. His bedroom began to resemble The Somme. Transparent, bloodless limbs filled his chest of drawers; wan severed heads lined his bookcase proudly like ancestral hunting trophies. Because that's what he was now – a hunter. A creature of the night. The 6th Earl of Newport Pagnelshire was now a royal vampire.

Once the initial shock had subsided, Anthony began to see the advantages of his new found bloodsucking. For the first time in his life, he had discovered a purpose. Each day required prey. He looked upon his old philosophy mater with new respect and remembered him quoting Heidegger. Twelve years too late, he understood the true meaning of existential responsibility. True, he couldn't disclose his secret to anybody but he had the magnificent responsibility of feeding. If he didn't feed; he'd die.

It was one Saturday afternoon, as he slurped down the last dregs of a homeless accordion player he found in Chancery Lane, that events took an unexpected turn. His manservant, Abdul, took a telephone call and informed Anthony that The Palace was on the line. Bored by the obvious hoax, Anthony decided to play along with the sport but his mood quickly changed when he heard the voice on the other end. Could it really be?

"Anthony old boy. Long time no speak. We're in a bit of a fix old Bean. We've got the Belgian ambassador staying for the weekend. Frightful bore but his pretty little niece is with him and she's a fine filly. She wants to do The Proms tonight. Normally we'd get Harry but he's nursing a cunt of a hangover. It won't be too arduous. She's a fruity little minx and it's only four hours of Wagner or some other Kraut. What say you?"

And so it was that four hours later, Anthony was sitting cheekily in a box at The Royal Albert Hall with a perfectly formed continental cutie. Even better, the bar was filled with paparazzi, acting on a tip off that the Prince was likely to show up with a beautiful Belgian bun. Anthony thought all his lottery numbers had come up in one night. He'd make the press and then he's have an hour of boning a Belgian before drinking her silly. Impromptu, he stroked her neck in anticipation for the feast to follow. All his life, Anthony had suffered from premature ejaculation and it was one of life's more galling tricks that this carried over into his bloodsucking as well. As the woodwind section built to a crescendo, he could hold off no longer, and sunk his teeth into her firm, rosy flesh. Naturally, she screamed out and it drew attention away from the tenor hitting a bum note. Thinking on his feet, whilst siphoning off a few pints of the red stuff into his hip flask, he rang the bell for the waiter. As luck would have it, on duty was Frank, an ageing waiter, whose claim to fame is that he appeared on Top of The Pops in 1974 as a Womble. Frank dropped his tray but Anthony floored him and kept him pinned down until security arrived. The staunch opera lovers amongst the audience were a bit miffed but for the majority, this drama taking place in the Royal box was riveting. Frank was arrested for "vampiral offenses" and Anthony was carried from the theatre aloft and hailed as a modern day Van Helsing. Guess what all the Sunday papers ran with the next day.

It would be wonderful to end the story there – a wastrel finally becomes a national celebrity. But that would be overlooking the fact that, for vampires, every day brings fresh challenges and one can never rest for long on one's own laurels.

Amongst the family, the full truth of Anthony's habits started to emerge. But one of the advantages of being a Royal is that you are provided with members of the royal protection squad. These silent figures are usually unattached men (or women), whose sudden disappearance is unlikely to cause too great an alarm. Occasionally, a staff from the masters of the rolls team would have to deal with a tearful auntie from Dorset, desperate to trace her nephew who had left so proudly two months ago to take up his royal posting. But all in all, hushing things up was easy peasy for the family. Nobody would have noticed the sizeable increase in luggage as the family set off for Balmoral but it was truly a wonderful place to dispose of 365 bloodless security officers. All those glens that nobody has access to, and if the bones are dug up in a few years time, well, we can always blame Culloden.

Was it Heidegger who said "If you try hard enough and hang in there long enough, fame and riches will come your way. Even if it means succumbing to a life of immortality and a daily piercing of people's necks". What a funny old world it is.

In A State

February 15, 2013

The other day, a good friend of mine was describing his adventures on the S&M scene and talking about how he loves adopting a totally submissive role, completely under the control of his mistress. This was quite a surprise as, he would be the first to admit, he is such a control freak in every aspect of his life. He will actively avoid situations if it means he won't be completely in control.

I'm very much like that myself (minus the whips and handcuffs) and yet nearly every aspect of my life is under some sort of control by the State. I can make the minor, everyday decisions (liver or chops for tea?) but the State involvement in the major areas of my life has been, and is still, immense. It made me realise again how much the consequences of being a carer, go against my natural psychological instinct – it's no wonder that I find things unbearable at times. This isn't a moan post; more an account of how life is when you're caring for an adult full time. Let's look at the main areas of my (or any human's) life:

Marriage
The State effectively ended my marriage (or at least put it on hold whilst I remain Steven's carer). To be told that if I remain in my marriage, our son would be removed from our care is a terrible choice to have to make. Wife or son? It really was as stark as that.

Family:
Needless to say, there was the massive interference to my family life in 2010 when Steven was kept away from his home for the whole of 2010. Furthermore, the State's plan was to move him further away from home on a permanent basis and the care plan was that we could have webcam contact. If they had got their way, that would have been the end of my family life.

Relationships:
I'm not particularly in the market for a relationship at the moment but even if I was, it would be impossible to build one. I get every other Monday evening off from my caring role. I also get 2 hours on Tuesday mornings (which is housework time) and 1 1/2 hours on Friday evening (which is paperwork time). I can't see a potential partner being too chuffed about such limited, controlled contact. The same applies with my friends; if I want to meet up with them it has to be within the schedule determined by the State.

Work:
At present, I can work between 21 and 24 hours per week. I wouldn't be able to hold down a 9 to 5 job because I don't have the support package to enable it. I'd like to work more hours than I do and there have been quite a few occasions over the past four years where I have been offered work opportunities but had to pass them over as I couldn't give them the time commitment necessary. So, my opportunities to develop a meaningful career are in the hands of Panel; that vague bunch of people who decide on support packages.

Finance:
Obviously, the restrictions on the time I can work has a big impact on my finances and most days my main meal is something on toast. The only state benefit I claim is housing benefit and that is so stressful, I'd love to work more, earn more and not be reliant on it. Now that I have been appointed Steven's court deputy, the court wants full records of how I spend his money, and likewise, because Hillingdon want to keep an eye out that I don't spend his money in order to contrive him getting social housing for Steven, they want to see detailed accounts of his expenditure too. It's the same with direct payments. I don't know where the idea of choice and flexibility comes from; Steven's direct payments are meticulously calculated and can only be used to cover the wages of the support workers. I'm not allowed to use the direct payments for anything else and have to produce masses of paperwork to prove that.

Home:
As I've documented many times, where we live and even if we have a home to live in at all is controlled by the Local Authority. The State will shortly hear my housing benefit appeal and if that goes against us, the LA have stated they won't rehouse Steven because of his damages award. That will mean, the State will have to move Steven into residential care and I will be homeless. This is not the choice I would make if I had the choice.

Marriage, family, relationships, home, work, finances – basically the foundations stones to anyone's life. One thing I am pleased about is that I was able to find the balls and stand up to the LA and stop doing all those endless logs they were so insistent on. To have every action of Steven's life (and by default, mine) scrutinised and judged was one control too many.

Perhaps I should pop along to Miss Kinky's Dildo Emporium and treat myself to some handcuffs and a whip. They might come in handy for my next carer's assessment review.

The Unsung Carer

Hello. My name is Mark Neary and I'm a Carer. This is my introduction every week at my carer's anonymous meetings.

After the court case, I jointly founded a group called the Carers Solidarity Group. It has been both a lifeline but a source of annoyance as well. The carer is so unheard, so devalued that trying to have a voice is pretty pointless. Nobody is interested.

Included in this section, is a guest post I wrote for Lucy Series' blog "The Small Places". It followed some research I was involved in with the CSG and the biggest disappointment about it, besides the utterly depressing results, was that we couldn't get anyone in the media interested in it. Once a year is National carers week and for the other 51 weeks, we are humoured and ignored.

- Great: It's National Carer's Week
- What Price Carer's Assessments

Great – It's National Carers Week

June 18, 2012

That rather muted fanfare you heard this morning may have been heralding the start of this year's National Carer's Week. The annual event where the lives and needs of carers are in the spotlight (that may mean a three minute slot on Daybreak, squeezed between the weather report and Ross King's latest news from a Hollywood red carpet). The big charities will talk about the lack of funding, the impact of caring on the carer's health. Carers will be praised for their stoicism and the word of the week will probably be "unsung".

What's it like to be one of the unsung? In 2008, I was given a holiday by the Princess Royal's Trust for Carers. I was very grateful and it was a brilliant week, even if the venue (Pontins in Blackpool) had been stuck in 1973, since 1973. What struck me as much as the stoicism and sheer doggedness of all the holidaymakers, was what a bedraggled lot we were. It put me in mind of that last scene of The Posseidon Adventure, when the survivors emerge from the ship. If you want a good working definition of the phrase "at the end of one's tether", go to a carer's holiday. It's hard to buy the latest designer labels in swimwear out of your Carers Allowance. But there was a fantastic atmosphere, in a Cameronish, we're all in this together, sort of way.

I feel rather pessimistic about this year's Carer's week. Over the last year, I've noticed a change in attitude towards the disabled and the people who care for them. On a good day, you might get apathy but on a bad day, thanks in no small measure to those great champions of the disabled like Maria Miller and Ian Duncan Smith, you get downright hostility. And when the mood swings from apathy to hostility, it's hardly the greatest background to bring about some kind of change.

Earlier this year, the Carers Solidarity group that I'm a member of, produced a report about the shocking use (or mis-use?) of the carers grant and how carers assessments are conducted across the country. Statisticians could pour over the report for hours but the bottom line was simple; the will isn't there and the money that is available, is not being made available to carers. I was naive. I thought that after the media coverage I got for the Neary vs Hillingdon case last year, this report might get a bit of coverage. Sadly it didn't, although a lady in Newport Pagnell tutted! Apathy. Or perhaps we chose a week to release the report at a time when Katie Price was having some relationship difficulties. I've blogged about it before but here are two statistics: 64% of the money LAs receive from Central Government for a Carers Grant do not get through to carers (and we're talking millions here). 72% of carers assessments carried out don't actually lead to anything whatsoever for the carer. Can anyone think of a more pointless (and expensive) activity than that?

The bee in my bonnet is respite. After months and months of haggling, I've finally got it agreed that I can receive 42 nights of respite a year. As my son is still traumatised by his previous experience of respite, where he was carted off after one day to a positive behaviour unit, and didn't return home for a year, we have our respite at home. A carer arrives at 6pm; I go out and meet friends or sit in a pub on my own and write blogs, come home about 10 and the carer takes charge if any caring is needed during the night. It works and it is cheap at £65 per night. Couldn't the provision of respite be mandatory – the actual content of it, dependent on the circumstances. The respite arrangement has been a lifesaver to me, much more than a nice spa or an Indian head massage once a year might have been. Wouldn't it be fabulous if this kind of arrangement was there for everybody who needed it. The money is there; the will isn't.

I know I'm being fanciful but I'd love National Carers week to produce something as concrete and useful as a statutory respite provision. The chances of that happening are less than zero but as a valuable alternative, we may all be offered, a person centred chiropody session.

The fanfare can stop now. Carers Week will be all over in six days.

What Price Carers Assessments

Over the past couple of years, I have become more and more interested in how the idea of a false reality (or false consciousness) that is prevalent in much of our lives today, has become such a central part of the adult social care world. Why is that when I am told "we are acting in your best interests", does my reality feel that is someone else's best interests that are being served. Why, when my son is asked to participate in the drawing up of his own person centred plan and must come up with a wish list, are all the items on his wish list rejected as "unsuitable or inappropriate". Why, am I constantly being told that individual budget are all about "choice and flexibility" and then discover that I have only one option for respite. Why, after selling me direct payments as "user and carer empowerment", do I feel thoroughly dis-empowered?

Perhaps the biggest challenge to my perception of my reality is the issue of carers assessments. Mr Cameron, Mr Clegg and Mr Milliband have all spoken out about the "valuable role" of carers and how "we must recognise the role that carers play". As this research shows, this is surely a case of words speaking louder than actions. But there is a cruelty too. By presenting the carer with the opportunity of a carers assessment, an expectation is set up that the carer may be about to receive some respect and have their needs valued. A couple of months ago, the BBC published details of an Ipsos Mori survey for cancer research that revealed that 49% of carers receive no support at all. The BBC report concluded with the following quote: "David Rogers, chair of the Local Government Association's Community Wellbeing Board, said: "As this report highlights, the sad reality is that many carers don't recognise themselves as such and fail to seek the support to which they are rightly entitled, and which is widely available through their local authority." There is a double whammy in that statement: Firstly, it suggests that the fault is with the carer for not identifying themselves as a carer. Most carers that I come across know exactly that they are a carer. And, actually Mr Rogers it is the job of the authority to identify their carers and offer an assessment. Secondly, after failing to recognise that we are carers, we then make the secondary mistake of not knowing what support is available. Even, widely available. And it is that last statement; that false reality, that this piece seeks to expose and address.

In the last five years, I have participated in four carers assessments. They have been conducted by four different social workers (or carers champions, or carers services co-ordinators) but the script each time is identical. I have seen Blood Brothers four times, with Kiki Dee, then Stephanie Lawrence, then Linda Nolan and finally Melanie C in the lead role. Four different actresses but they all say the same lines and sing the same songs. A carers assessment works along the same lines:

"Would some counselling help with your burden of being a carer?"

"Possibly. I'm a counsellor myself actually but......"

"I can give you some numbers of some counselling organisations".

"Will the carer's assessment lead to some funding with that?"

"Er – no. But you can always ask your GP for a referral to the NHS counselling service...."

The outcome of these assessments (and they are usually a good 90 minutes long) is that I come away with lots of phone numbers; leaflets on the importance of a good diet and a good night's sleep and ..... nothing else. On each occasion, I have brought up that respite might be useful but each time have been told, that respite isn't part of the carers assessment remit – that comes under the caree's needs assessment. (I've never understood that one; surely it is the carer who needs the respite)

Six months ago, I discovered that local authorities receive an annual carer's grant from central government to provide services and support for carers. Across the country, these grants average about £1.7 million per council. My first thought upon this discovery was: where is the money going? I've heard stories of carers being offered free one off Indian head massage sessions; a free day's horse riding lesson; even a weekend course in kite flying. But all these activities seemed small change when I found out the sums involved in the carers grant.

Around this time, I was invited to join an online group called the Carers Solidarity Group. It was suggested that we make our first project an investigation into the way local authorities distribute their carer's grants. The naive aim was to find out what money is available so we could inform carers of their rights and options prior to undertaking a carer's assessment. We also decided to look at the outcomes of carers assessments to clarify if they actually produce anything concrete for the carer. The results of this research drive this blog post.

Freedom of information requests were sent to over 60 local authorities. I've attached two tables: the first showing how much of the carers grant is allocated to carers; the second reveals how many carer's assessments produce anything worthwhile for the carer:

Carers Grants

The % figure shows how much of the carers grant was given to carers or carer's organisations. The total grant is shown in brackets

0% = Enfield (£1.585,000)

0% = Glasgow City (£429,000)

0% = Kensington & Chelsea (£936,000)

0% = Kingston (£500,000)

0% = Lewisham (£1,726,000)

2.8% = Bexley (£991,447)

3.4% = Wandsworth (£1,466,000)

6.8% = Durham (£2,836,000)

6.9% = Merton (£685,700)

8% = Hammersmith & Fulham (£1,419,000)

15.7% = Haringey (£1.405,700)

15.7% = Waltham Forest (£1,334,000)

17% = Bath & East Somerset (£2,809,085)

18.1% = Wirral (£1,585,500)

20% = Liverpool (£2,806,800)

21.6% = Islington (£1,444,000)

29.6% = Leeds (£3,528,170)

32% = City of London (£31,000)

32.6% = Devon (£3,654,000)

33.4% = Newham (£984,000)

35% = Northamptonshire (£2,807,000)

35.9% = Hackney (£1,853,000)

36% = Barking (£1,135,749)

36.4% = Barnet (£1,125,000)

38% = Harrow (£1,099,000)

38,7% = Cheshire East (£1,436,000)

41.8% = Greenwich (£1,676,000)

43% = Bradford (£2,691,000)

44.8% = Bromley (£1,291,000)

50.4% = Richmond (£681,000)

53.5% = Kent (£6,242,000)

55.7% = Knowsley (£1,071,000)

59% = Croydon (£1,666,000)

66.4% = Medway (£1,039,000)

66.6% = Sutton (£1,402,000)

69% = Ealing (£1,622,221)

70% = Surrey (£4,700,000)

76.8% = Norfolk (£4,600,000)

77% = Hillingdon (£1,054,956)

81% = Swansea (£787,100)

88.4% = Westminster (£3,866,000)

92.6% = Tower Hamlets (£1,425,500)

102% = Lambeth (£1,839,922)

The following councils refused to answer some or all of the questions: Essex, Havering, Hounslow, Manchester, Redbridge, South Bucks, Southwark, Windsor & Maidenhead

Carers Assessments:

The % figure shows how many carers assessments produced either a weekly payment or one off payment to meet a carer's need. The total number of assessments carried out is in brackets.

0% = Bexley (1170)

0% = Glasgow (773)

0.5% = Medway (707)

0.6% = Hillingdon (1236)

0.7% = Isle of Anglesey (414)

0.8% = Kent (20,820)

1.2% = Barking (2110)

1.4% = Hammersmith & Fulham (654)

2.8% = Durham (5040)

3% = Bromley (1705)

3% = Northamptonshire (884)

3.3% = Enfield (1292)

3.8% = Swansea (2053)

5.8% = Essex (8465)

6% = Barnet (1868)

7.7% = Bath & East Somerset (1462)

8.5% = Knowsley (1956)

11.3% = Kingston (935)

11.7% = Greenwich (1042)

12% = Norfolk (6724)

12.5% = Newham (864)

13% = Hounslow (802)

13% = Merton (1321)

14% = Liverpool (2450)

16% = Harrow (3094)

16.8% = Ealing (918)

20% = Bournemouth (920)

24% = Leeds (2584)

25% = Devon (4539)

26% = Croydon (766)

28% = Cheshire East (1579)

28% = Bradford (4245)

31.7% = Sutton (1027)

34% = Lambeth (1487)

36% = Islington (1115)

36.7% = Richmond (718)

51.6% = Lewisham (1472)

55% = Wandsworth (760)

58.6% = Hackney (685)

66.5% = Waltham Forest (430)

82% = Southwark (149)

91% = Surrey (1552)

99% = Tower Hamlets (486)

108% = Haringey (649)

128% = Manchester (2262)

242% = City of London (26)

We asked five main questions:
1. How much was your carers grant from central government for 2010/11?
2. How much of this carer's grant was allocated directly to carers or given to external organisations with a remit of supporting carers?
3. How many carer's assessments were carried out in 2010/11?

4. How many carer's assessments identified a need that led to the carer receiving regular direct payments and/or a personal budget?
5. How many carers' assessments identified a need that led to the carer receiving a one off payment to meet that need?

Before reviewing the results, it is important to acknowledge some flaws in the information we received:

1. Many councils have set up sub services with names like "Carers support centre" that have the initial appearance of being an external agency. Upon further investigation, we learned these were in house teams and money was siphoned from the carers grant to fund these teams in areas like staff salaries, recruitment, tendering costs. So, we feel it is a reasonable assumption that at least a proportion of the money allocated to these services probably didn't reach the carer.
2. Some external agencies received substantial carers grant allocations for specific services they provide (e.g. respite, counselling etc). However, we discovered that often, these agencies will charge for that service which raises the question: what exactly are the carers grant being used for. For example, Norfolk council gave a considerable portion of its grant to Crossroads Care for respite services. However, several group members have reported that if you approach Crossroads, having been pointed in that direction by the council, you discover there is quite a large charge for the service. This has led service users to believe that a significant portion of the grant must be used to cover salaries, admin, accommodation etc. Further FOI requests to each organisation would have to be made to clarify this further.

Flaws aside, the research still yielded some valuable and shocking information. Here are a couple of bald statistics:

1. Of the 42 councils who responded, only 36% of the total carer's grant they received was allocated to carers. (Bearing in mind the flaws mentioned in 1 above, this figure is almost certainly a lot lower. 64% of approx £54 million is not reaching carers.

2. Five councils allocated **none** of their carers grant to carers. The average grant is £1,375 million.
3. 26 of the 42 councils, had a less than 20% success rate in providing anything worthwhile for the carer following a carers assessment.

Sadly, it seems that carer's assessments for a lot of local authorities are a tick box exercise. Take Hillingdon Council; in 2010/11, it carried out 1236 carer's assessments, which on paper looks a very laudable achievement. If my experience is anything to go, that equates to roughly 1850 man hours. However, after spending all that time, energy and paperwork, only **8** carers benefited with a regular direct payment or one off payment. For the other 1228, their carer's assessment must have been pretty pointless as the assessment produced absolutely nothing. (By the way, I'm due my next carer's assessment in a few weeks and I'm determined to be number 9 and accept a fish foot spa that I don't really want!) It is like the trick sell – we are meant to believe that the value is in having the assessment, whereas of course, any value is in whatever the outcome of the assessment.

Astonishingly, two councils, Bexley and Glasgow conducted 1943 carer's assessments between them, without producing a single outcome. A big fat 0% despite getting a combined carers grant of nearly £1.5 million. I hate to be cynical but I'd wager that the Bexley's carers champion has a very tastefully furnished office.

A note of caution should be expressed, even with the councils whose carer's assessments seemingly produce a high level of practical outcomes for carers. For example, Southwark council managed to provide 82% of the carers they assessed with direct payments or a one off payment. However, in 2010/11, they completed just 159 assessments. I think it is a reasonable assumption that there are many many carers in Southwark who don't even get out of the starting blocks and get offered a carers assessment.

Part of the problem is that often, carer's needs are conflated with their caree's needs when in fact they have two entirely separate needs. In my case, my son is being offered two nights away from home each month – this comes under a need identified in his assessment of "facilitating his independence". To the council, this is respite, whether it meets my need or not. It would make more sense if the carer and their caree's needs were assessed independently of each other.

Clearly, by far the biggest problem is that there is a lot of money being passed around that carers don't even get a sniff of. Unhelpfully, the carers grant isn't ring-fenced, so it is quite possible that the carer may be desperate for a break from caring but that break is unavailable but your city centre Christmas decorations look fabulous. Wouldn't it be fantastic if all carers walked into their assessment knowing exactly how much money was available and they can cost a service that will meet their need. My local council received a carer's grant of £1,054,956 in 2010/11. I have costed a reasonable respite package for myself at £3900 per annum. If I'm lucky, I may get it. If every carer reading this research uses the information herein, we may not be brought off with bingo evenings for much longer.

As I said at the start of this piece, we often hear platitudes from politicians, commending carers for the valuable job they do. In order for actions to speak louder than words, three things need to happen:

1. Carer's assessments must be taken more seriously. They cannot be a tick box exercise, used to justify a ideology or create a false reality that something of value may come to the carer as a result of the assessment. They must be meaningful.
2. Authorities must be more transparent about the money they receive and what is available for the carer. I'm quite capable of identifying my own needs and I'm even capable of finding and costing a package to meet those needs. The Authority can always say "no" to my proposal but at

least, the process isn't the covert process we find today. I might actually feel empowered.

3. A carer's assessment must be seen as a valuable item in its own right, not just an adjunct to their caree's assessment. The needs may overlap but too often, we are presented with the false reality of being helped, because our caree is being helped but in fact, we are receiving no help at all.

Court Out

The saga over Steven's damages dragged on and on. I wasn't that bothered about them but all the advice I got was that Steven should be compensated for his nightmare of 2010. Fair enough. It took over 18 months from the court case to get them and there were many hurdles in the way, along the way:

- Damages Limitations
- Bed
- You're My Favourite Deputy

Damages Limitations (or "All I Want Is a New Sodding Bed")

November 5, 2012

On 26th July 2012, Steven was awarded damages by the Court of Protection following Justice Peter Jackson's ruling in June 2011 that Steven had been illegally deprived of his liberty for a whole year in 2010. The official solicitor had tried to negotiate a damages package with the Defendant for over nine months but, as has been the case since Steven was first held by Hillingdon, this proved impossible and so the matter had to come before the court again. So, it has been 17 months since the original judgement and four months since the damages ruling and Steven is still as far as ever from receiving the award.

For the first time today, I got a copy of the judgement. It states that "the defendant shall pay to the claimant the sum of £35000 in full and final settlement of his claim, inclusive of interest, such payment to be made within 28 days of the date of the order herein". I only received the order as I asked the solicitor for a supporting letter to provide to the bank to try to arrange a bank loan to buy Steven a new bed. I am repairing the current bed about twice a week but it must be bloody hard for him to sleep properly in a Heath Robinson contraption.

It seems like the delay is caused by the OS's application for me to become Steven's welfare deputy and that the money won't be released until the court agrees to me taking on that role. That sounds fine and I'm more than happy to do that. However, so far, it has been fraught with difficulties:

- Steven had to have a mental capacity assessment to determine that he doesn't have the capacity to manage his own affairs. I wrote about that experience in a previous blog but it has transpired that the doctor failed to complete the whole form, so it had to be returned to her for completion.
- I had to complete and sign a "notification" form that stated I had explained to Steven what is happening and that he agrees to it. I did this the day after receiving the form two weeks ago but was told today that the forms have never been received so have to go through it all again.
- Steven was awarded legal aid when the order was granted in July but legal aid has a time limit on it and that has now expired (without anything happening), so he's had to reapply all over again.

Today is the deadline for getting all the forms back to the Court of Protection. And then what?

Nothing is ever easy.

And all he wants is a new sodding bed

Bed

December 3, 2012

Sorry. My apologies. This is another post about the nightmare of being caught up in systems. Systems that are about support. And by God, I've got a full house of systems: the social care system; the benefits system; the legal system. You name a system and it's probably playing a part in controlling my life.

I've never felt so physically unwell as I have in the last two months since the housing benefit problem blew up. I am permanently exhausted; I've passed out twice recently and I've lost about a stone in weight. I've seen the doctor and had the blood tests, and apart from high blood pressure, they can't find anything else untoward, so it has to be the stress I've been going through. For the first time in my life, at the age of 52, I've been worried about my health.

This morning, I had a fantastic guided meditation with a friend and I was shocked by her summing up: "It's appalling Mark. In the last four years, Hillingdon have threatened every single human right you can name". In 2009, they brought about the end of my marriage by making me chose between my wife and my son. In 2010, they breached my son's (and therefore mine as well) right to a family life by keeping him away from his home for a year. Now, through their vindictive (a barrister's word) interpretation of the housing benefit regulations, they are compromising my home. And throughout the four years, they have abruptly cancelled Steven's support package so many times, they have stopped me working. (I did a rough calculation and I've probably lost about £22,000 in earnings since I've been entrapped by the support system). Marriage, family, home, work – pretty fundamental things and all lost or screwed up because I got caught up in the system.

I've got a chance next year of earning, for me, a considerable amount of money for a time investment that will fit in with my caring responsibilities. I have 90 minutes free on a Friday night and my plan last Friday was to get cracking on the proposal for this project. However, I got home from work to find an email from the brilliant barrister who has been instructed to deal with the housing benefit problem. It needed a reply that obviously took priority over anything else. On Saturday, I get an interrupted two hours whilst Steven does a music session, so adjourned the business project until then. Only, that two hours was taken up having to reply to Hillingdon's nonsensical response to my appeal; it was completely pointless but unavoidable and another two hours wasted to the system. Tomorrow, I have another two hours free in the morning whilst Steven goes to his water aerobics but our bath is leaking water through the light fitting in the living room. Today, Steven got an electric shock and the lights fused, so that time tomorrow will be spent dealing with the plumber. And that's it; the 5 1/2 hours when I'm not either caring or working has gone and the business proposal, which could lead to me being almost self-sufficient and away from some of the systems, is put to bed for another week.

The other system that I'm finding difficult right now is the legal system, even though it has been my saviour for the past two years. It's 18 months since our court case and Steven still hasn't been paid his damages; he has to wait until I'm appointed his financial and affairs deputy and goodness knows when that will come through. His bed is broken; I can't swap it with mine as mine is even more broken than his. I have been asking the solicitor for months if a tiny amount of his damages can be released to buy a new bed but I've been told that the money cannot be made available until after the hearing. I've been praised by a high court judge for my commitment to my son but I'm not trusted with a few hundred pounds of his damages until I'm rubber stamped by the court. Another system.

Have you noticed that none of this is about Steven. Despite the meltdowns and the fact that his December anxiety ("Not going on a break to M House after Christmas") has kicked in early this year, looking after Steven is chicken feed compared to the stress caused by being in the support systems. Steven has now been home for 707 days and I've not had a problem with him in those 707 days that I cannot handle; I wish I could say the same for the external input.

I have made a decision though. As soon as the damages are paid out, we're moving away from Hillingdon. That may be fraught with difficulties and could be a case of out of the frying pan into the fire, but nothing can be as bad as we've experienced the last four years. My marriage has gone; I'll never be able to earn a decent living but I may be able to hold what's left of my family together. If my health holds, it may even be quite exciting. I can even make a good best interests decision for Steven for the move, despite the upheaval.

Last week, I didn't go to my best mate's wedding. As my housing benefit has been stopped, I couldn't afford to lose two days work and pay a support worker for an overnight and some extra daytime hours. I hope our relationship gets through his disappointment and my shame at letting him down. That's what life in the system is all about.

You're My Favourite Deputy

January 16, 2013

At last. I've received the paperwork from the Court of Protection informing me that I have been officially appointed as Steven's property and affairs deputy. No sealed order yet and no damages award yet; they have to wait until I put up a surety in case I abscond to Barbados with the proceeds of Steven's compensation. Will I be able to take him on holiday for his birthday in March? Will he eventually get his new bed by the spring? Who knows but for the first time since Justice Jackson's ruling in June 2011, it feels like we're moving in the right direction.

In the past couple of months, I've been on my soapbox in the blog posts "Straight From The Gut" about what I see as the flaws in the mental capacity assessment. In particular, I have questioned their almost sole reliance on cognitive decision-making and paying scant attention to the way that most people make their decisions by referring to their gut instinct, feelings or previous experience. And for people with communication difficulties, even if they are able to make a purely cognitive decision, they may struggle to communicate how they did it. I watched Steven the other day after I'd told him about a change to our routine next Friday. There was a lot of mental activity going on and from his response, I had correctly guessed that he was doing three things:

- Absorbing the information I had given him.
- Working out how the change would impact on him.
- Deciding what alternative plan he'd like in place.

Basically, it was about me doing the weekly shop next Thursday evening instead of next Friday morning as I need to get up to London by 10am on the Friday. There were two aspects of this that would impact Steven: would he get his cheese on toast that we make together when I get back from Sainsburys and would he get to watch his Men Behaving Badly DVD that I cue up for him before I go shopping? It took him about 10 minutes before he said: "Have cheese on toast for supper on Thursday night", followed by, "Dad do Men Behaving Badly and then go on the train on Friday". Brilliant, but if he had to explain how he'd reached these conclusions, he'd struggle.

Whilst reading through the CoP paperwork, it struck me that I may have had an un-necessary bee in my bonnet; certainly in terms of the mental capacity act.

The guidance I've received about assessing decision-making capacity states that: "people have the right to make unwise decisions"; "people have the right to make wrong decisions", and "consider any values, views, beliefs, wishes and **feelings** they may have expressed". I was shocked on reading this as it hasn't been my experience of Steven's previous assessments. In 2010, social services had decided what the "right" decision was, about where Steven should live. The very matey referral letter ("How's the family? We must meet up for lunch sometime") from the social work manager to the assessing psychiatrist hardly opened the field for him considering anything other than the "right" decision. What chance did Steven have to present an alternative view under these conditions? Where was the consideration of Steven's values, views, wishes and feelings?

So, perhaps the problem is not with the ACT as I'd thought but with the way in which it has been implemented by some of the professionals. Perhaps the Act offers the scope for the learning disabled that I've been calling for. Perhaps the problem is with the risk averse system, or the pig-headed "we know best" system. Remember the Cardiff case about the elderly lady who wanted to go on her annual cruise with her partner. The LA thought this was an unwise decision, too risky and subsequently slapped a deprivation of liberty order on her. A judge lifted the order and off she went. I never read any news reports of her falling overboard, so presumably the holiday went well. None of the stress or costly court hearing needed to happen if the code of practice had been applied fairly. I find it terrifying that I might, in the future, have my fundamental life decisions made by people who won't allow me, out of risk or through an absolute certainty of their rightness, the grace of using my feelings, my instinct or my previous experience to choose how I live my life.

There are several references in the code of practice to appointing an IMCA when there are difficulties. And we all know how difficult it is to get an IMCA if the LA don't want you to have one. If the decision maker believes their decision is the absolute right decision, they are not going to very open to having a second opinion. This is a massive challenge for people in the field and for people who come under the Act. Can you listen to; understand; and not discriminate against the learning disabled person when there are decisions about their life to be made.

One other thing that came out of reading about my responsibilities as a deputy is the code of practice confirms my thoughts about the conflict of interests in the decision I'm being forced to make over my housing benefit. Regular readers of this blog will know that Hillingdon want me to transfer my tenancy into Steven's name and then he'll have to meet the rental liability out of his damages. The code clearly identifies this as a conflict of interests and the solution is to either appoint an IMCA or take the matter to the Court of Protection. With Hillingdon, it feels like I'm in an interminable chess match, so I've written to them asking them to make an IMCA referral. And what will the court make of Hillingdon bringing about this conflict of interests? Should be interesting.

I had to sign a court form, confirming that I'd explained my deputy role to Steven. His reaction? – "Dad's a deputy like Woody in Toy Story". As much as I like Pixar's cowboy, I'd prefer to be known as Steven's property and affairs space ranger. After all, since I got on the wrong side of them, I see my battles with Hillingdon continuing to infinity and beyond.

Inspired By Others

I get very embarrassed when I meet people and they talk about me as "an inspiration". I'm far more comfortable with having people inspire me. This section is a collection of writings that have been inspired by the writings or actions of others:

- Fear, Domination & Pepperoni Pizza
- Home Sweet Institution
- Consultation But Mind The Elephants

Fear, Domination and Pepperoni Pizza

November 2, 2012

Last month, Lucy Series posted an excellent blog about the Domination Theory that exists in social care (http://thesmallplaces.blogspot.co.uk/2012/09/the-problem-of-domination-in-social-care.html). The crux of the matter basically being that by the very nature of the social care system, there will always be a power imbalance. It is not a personal thing; the service user or carer is probably not being targeted but they will always have the fear of their life being completely disrupted by a decision taken by the social care team.

It struck a lot of nerves at the time of reading and I don't like the idea of being dominated. It's probably why I get into so many battles with the LA because I cannot bear to feel so powerless.

It shows up for me in the most unlikely places. This morning I did the weekly shop at Sainsburys. Money is very tight at the moment (I have to phone the gas board later as they want to put my monthly direct debit up to £195!!). On Fridays, Steven goes to a day centre run by the positive behaviour unit. A few months back, as part of Steven's "independence planning", the OT suggested that Steven make his own pizza whilst at the day centre and he can bring it home with him for tonight's tea. We had week's of observational monitoring forms to complete as every step of the pizza making process was analysed from a behavioural perspective. The support workers had to rate Steven's performance on every step of the task from 0-5. It was very tense for Steven and the support workers as they were being observed all the time whilst engaged in the pizza. Now it is just part of the Friday routine.

Whilst wheeling my trolley around, I added up the cost of making this pizza and it came to £7.65. A ready-made pepperoni pizza was on the shelves for £2.25. I could have saved myself £5.40. But I didn't because of fear; fear that I will be accused of being uncooperative in promoting Steven's independence. It's happened before in court and I live with the anxiety that it may happen again. And I feel pretty pathetic.

Home Sweet Institution

November 26, 2012

Last week at The Small Places blog, Lucy Series wrote a brilliant post about the challenges on people's human rights if they are living in an institutional setting. How the rights and choices, that those of us not living in care homes take for granted, go out of the window, no matter how benign or enlightened the culture of the care home may be.

It made me think about Steven's time at the positive behaviour unit in 2010 and how much of his usual life had to be compromised. he was expected to be tolerant of a whole set of rules that simply don't apply at home; not because I don't set rules but because they are not needed in the home environment. And those rules required Steven to be empathic to other residents, to the staff, to the ideologies of the local authority and as we know, autism and empathy don't normally go together. By the way, this post isn't meant to be a criticism of the unit; it's just an examination of how much a person gives up when they enter a care home. I reject though the comparison that other s have made between life in a care home with the communal living, with a group of students living together. As someone wrote on Twitter, a student is not going to have their lecturer enter their flat and tell them they can't drink, can't smoke or have sex.

Back to the positive behaviour unit and the first thing that both Steven and I found difficult was that the resident's guests weren't allowed in their rooms. The first time I visited Steven there he led me off to his room but the next day I received an email from the manager to say that it was prohibited. He gave two reasons: preserving the privacy of the other residents and ensuring my safety. I never understood that; we were going to Steven's room, not the other resident's. And as to my safety, that seemed to stem from their risk averse culture and bore no relation to the relationship I have with Steven. So, not being allowed to share quality, private time in his room, my two hourly visits took place in the dining room. I used to visit on a Saturday afternoon and tried to stick to Steven's favourite routine from a Saturday afternoon when he's at home, which is a music session. So, I used to prepare a C90 tape and take along Steven's ghetto blaster for a familiar music session. Except that we were frequently joined by other residents, interested in what was going on. Or we'd be interrupted by staff coming to get the evening meal out of the freezer. Or by staff coming in to check on my safety! Each interruption would make Steven more agitated and I grew to loathe those visits. In every other relationship in my life, if I want to spend two private hours with that person, I can pretty much guarantee we could achieve that. And yet, I could never get it, with the most important in my life for just two hours a week because of the unit's rules and the needs of approximately twelve other people.

Another very problematic area during the year in the unit was bathtimes (I can't bear to use that institutional phrase "personal care"). Steven made it very clear that he was uncomfortable with women supervising his bathtime; reasonable for an awkward young man. Bear in mind that this job including someone applying his eczema cream to his private parts and it becomes even more understandable. However, Steven was at the mercy of the shift rotas and on many occasions there were only females on duty. Inevitably, this led to several of the incidents of "challenging behaviour" that the unit meticulously logged and which they used as their rationale for keeping him away from home. The solution was simple; send him home or respect his wishes. I am a man. His support workers at home are all male. But I was told that he had to accept a multi gender staff team. Can you imagine the outcry if any of the female readers of this blog expressed their discomfort about a man being in their bathroom, only to be told that it was okay for that man to apply soothing lotion to their breasts? No, of course, you can't imagine it because it would never happen. Person centred care goes down the plughole.

There were a lot of other examples. Here are a few:

- How do you explain to an autistic man who has watched Countdown every week day for the past fifteen years that he can only watch it once every four days because he has to take into account the viewing requirements of four other residents (and the staff – I remember Wimbledon fortnight when all the residents were in their rooms but all the staff were glued to the TV). Oh, and he can't have a TV in his room because bedrooms are out-of-bounds during the day.
- How do you explain to a young man in 2010 that he has no computer access and he has to forgo his three times a week Youtube session. This is complicated for the young autistic man as he can see there are three computers in the office that seem to be working fine. At home, if he suddenly decides he wants to watch the Fine Young Cannibals singing Johnny Come Home, he can because he has his own computer. Having a computer that is only used for spreadsheets about client behaviour patterns isn't something that is part of his normal life and he doesn't really get it.

- How do you explain to a young autistic man who in the past 15 years has been able to eat a whole bag of crisps once a day all to himself that he has to empty that one bag of crisps evenly into four bowls and be shared with the other residents? Whilst on the subject of food, I don't buy foods that I don't like. Or if I go into a restaurant and there's nothing on the menu I like, I walk straight out again. Unfortunately, in an institution, if you don't like the one dish on the menu, you go hungry.

I bought Steven a mobile phone whilst he was away but unfortunately, he couldn't get the hang of selecting from the four numbers I put in it. So, if he wanted to speak to me, his mother, his uncle, or his friend, he had to ask and wait for a phone or a member of staff to be free. And even then, he wasn't allowed in the office, so had to conduct a conversation in the main lounge in front of all the residents and staff.

I wrote in "Get Steven Home" about Steven's person centred plan. People who don't live in institutions don't have person centred plans; they have the freedom to be as person centred as they like and god forbid, not even have a plan in their lives. Steven came up with six things for his person centred wish list:

1. "Want to live in the Uxbridge house forever and ever".
2. "Want to open my Christmas presents in the Uxbridge house on Christmas Day".
3. "Want to go on holiday to Somerset".
4. "Want to have sausage and bacon in Rip's cafe".
5. "Want to go to Hampton outdoors swimming pool".
6. "Want to see Toy Story 3 at the cinema".

All six things were refused. Because they were passed through an institutional funnel. I'll never forget Justice Peter Jackson questioning the safeguarding manager about number (3): "So, you can't go on holiday if you're under a DoL? Really? Good heavens! I'm shocked!".

Needless to say, since Steven has been home we've done all six: you can express yourself and get your needs met without a person centred plan. Who'd have thought!

You might ask who was bothered by all this; me or Steven? Well, obviously by the tone of this post it bothered me (and still does). But, I witnessed Steven's agitation when our brief, valuable two-hour Take That session was repeatedly interrupted. I've read the umpteen incident reports, so have seen how problematic it was for him having a female do his bath. And since Steven has been home, he has never once chosen the Alan Titchmarch show on ITV1 over Countdown!

When I lived in a communal house, it was bedlam most of the time. Sometimes we were mature enough to negotiate. And I could stand my corner over expressing my wishes; I didn't have someone telling me that I lacked capacity to make a decision about what I wanted. If my fellow tenants wanted lasagne, I'd go out to the Wimpey Bar. I had total autonomy over who scrubbed my bollocks.

I've read this post back and clearly there are things that I am still angry about. But this isn't a rant post; I hope it's a post that adds a bit of flesh to the experience of institutional living. And perhaps illustrates that dead normal human rights are terribly difficult to uphold in an institution.

Consultation, But Mind the Elephants

August 1, 2012

There is a delicious juxtaposition of articles in my local paper today; the excellent Uxbridge Gazette.

The front page carries the story of the ongoing battle of a group of committed families to challenge the London Borough of Hillingdon's decision to close three of its day centres and replace them with one smaller "hub". The decision would mean that the number of people using the new centre would reduce by 50% and important relationships that have been built over several years will be lost forever. The families believe that the consultation process may have been unlawful and last week, permission was granted by the High Court for a full judicial review in September. Surprisingly, at the last-minute, the council have backtracked and have re-opened the consultation process. The article carries the headline: "Be open with us on day centre closures".

Flick over a couple of pages and we find the story of the High Court ruling last Thursday in the damages claim of Neary vs Hillingdon. Last week, a Court of Protection judge declared that Hillingdon should pay £35,000 to Steven for the year he was illegally detained in their care.

What strikes me as interesting about these two articles is the statement they make about Hillingdon's track record on consultation. In the original Neary Vs Hillingdon judgement June 2011, Justice Peter Jackson comments several times on the duplicity of the council; they led Steven and I to believe that Steven would be returning home, whilst behind the scenes, carrying out a quite different agenda of planning to move him hundreds of miles away. One of the reasons why the judge found that all four deprivation of liberty authorisations were unlawful was that they didn't record Steven's or my views. We were asked but our wishes were never included on the orders, much less acted upon. A superficial consultation. I know, from talking to the campaigners of the day centre closures, that the phrase "superficial consultation" is far too generous – the decision had long been made.

Another interesting feature of the two stories is the wonderful spin used by Hillingdon. In Steven's story, the deputy director of social care, Moira Wilson says, "The council is pleased a settlement has been reached which is satisfactory to the judge and the Neary family". The inference of this statement is that Hillingdon have been virtues of benevolence and that it has been the court and the Nearys that have caused the claim to take a year to reach settlement. A teensy weensy bit disingenuous Ms Wilson? For over a year, whatever figure the Official solicitor has proposed, Hillingdon have shrugged their shoulders apologetically and warned that they would have to claw back the damages by charging Steven the full rate for his care package. The claim could have been settled out of court without incurring any costs; there have been many opportunities over the last year for that to happen. Another needless hearing that will be added to the already enormous costs bill that Justice Jackson has ordered Hillingdon to bear. And there's another hearing to go. The Official Solicitor feels that because of the underhand way that Hillingdon have behaved all the way along, it is in Steven's best interests for me to be appointed his welfare deputy. It's a massive irony because Hillingdon sought to be appointed his welfare deputy back that first hearing in December 2010. Eighteen months later, they have shown themselves to be so untrustworthy that the Official Solicitor's position is that Steven needs extra protection from them for the future. Another costly hearing.

Back to the front page and the decision of the council to reopen the consultation process, the leader of the council, Mr Puddifoot speaks: "Whilst I have the greatest respect for those involved in the legal profession, I have no intention of allowing public funds, either from the legal aid budget or the council's social care budget, being utilised where it is not necessary". There you go then – take that you money grabbing solicitor bastards. You couldn't make this up!

Mr Puddifoot's statement exposes the almighty pickle councils get into when they make an "efficiency savings" decision and then try to present it as something completely different. There's no good reason to close three popular day centres other than money; yet it has been presented to the families as "promoting service user's independence". Hiding the real agenda is unsustainable and makes the illusory agenda ever more ludicrous. The same with Steven; every battle I have with the LA (whether it be about respite or the normal day-to-day care package) is about money but the discussions become farcical because we dare not speak money's name.

I don't see this ever changing because the truth can never be owned. So, in the meantime, public funds will continue to be utilised for legal fights in expensive court cases and day centres will continue to close and care packages will continue to be cut.

Scattergun Moaning

I can't find any other section to fit this next lot into, so perhaps I just have to accept that I'm an intolerant, bitter prat and be done with it:

- 16p To Fund A Respite Package
- Flexibility My Arse
- Trussed Up By Trust
- Ground Control to HMRC
- The Public Eye & The State Ear

16p To Fund A Respite Package

May 31, 2012

Dear Mr S

Re: Steven Neary: Respite Arrangement & Charges

I am having to write to you again as I arrived home from work today to find this month's direct payments remittance advice. Although, it was great to see an amount was included for the overnight respite that you agreed to in April, I was absolutely horrified to discover that Hillingdon are now levying a "client charge payable" at Steven. What this means in practice is absurd. You agreed to fund a respite package of 42 nights at £65 per night. The charge for both May and June were £129.84. That leaves me trying to fund a respite package for 16p!

What I find as hard to understand is that at no time during the long drawn out negotiations about the package was the subject of a charge ever mentioned. I have numerous letters and emails from yourself and other officers and I have attended many meetings where the subject of a charge has never been raised.

I feel totally hoodwinked. How on earth are we to carry out Justice Jackson's call to build a trusting relationship when yet again I have been misled? I cannot believe that not a single officer I have met over the past few months didn't know about the intention to charge Steven, so once again I have had important information withheld from me.

I draw your attention to paragraphs 95-96 in the Fairer Charging Guidance:

"Information about charges

95. Clear information about charges and how they are assessed should be readily available for users and carers. Local *Better Care, Higher Standards* charters should include this information. Information should be made available at the time a person's needs for care are assessed.

96. Once a person's care needs have been assessed and a decision has been made about the care to be provided, an assessment of ability to pay charges should be carried out promptly, and written information about any charges assessed as payable, and how they have been calculated, should be

communicated promptly. This should normally be done before sending a first bill. Charges should not be made for any period before an assessment of charges has been communicated to the user, although this may be unavoidable where the user has not co-operated with the assessment. A first bill for a charge for a lengthy past period can cause needless anxiety. Any increase in charges should also be notified and no increased charge made for a period before the notification".

What you have done seems to breach this policy on several counts:

1. I keep being informed that Steven is due to have a new needs assessment in preparation for a personal budget. So, this charge has been levied before a needs assessment has been completed.
2. No financial assessment has been carried out.
3. No written information has been communicated to me until today, and even then, only indirectly via the direct payments remittance advice.
4. You have charged Steven for May and June, which is before the charges have been communicated to us.
5. You have charged for a two month period prior to notification.

I am requesting the following:

1. The charges already deducted for May and June be reimbursed as soon as possible (i.e. Not wait until next month's DP are due).
2. No further charges are made until, firstly a new needs assessment is carried out, followed by a full financial assessment.

If this is not done, or the council are unwilling to rectify this, I wish this letter to be taken as an appeal against the decision to charge Steven for his care package without assessment, consultation or notification.

Finally, I would like to point out that although you agreed to the respite package in April, I have not been able to arrange any respite since then. Firstly, because the funds for May weren't paid until today and from now, I cannot obviously pay for respite at 16p a night.

I hope this matter receives your immediate attention.

Yours sincerely

Mark Neary

Flexibility, My Arse

November 12, 2012

Reasons why I don't like "flexible" direct payments and being an employer. Part 76.

This is going to sound a terribly unempathic post. My excuse is that it's not about the person who has triggered off the problem but the system that forces the situation on me.

Our main direct payment worker has gone long-term sick; he currently works 30.5 hours each week. Because he is an employee, he is entitled to sick pay. Having been self-employed since 1999, I have forgotten what it's like to have an automatic entitlement to sick pay – I've got used to the fact that if I don't work, I don't get paid. But as an employee, sick pay is part of the contract drawn up by the council, so I have to honour that.

The council's view is that I should budget out of the hourly rate to cover sick pay. But surely that doesn't apply if someone is long term sick. Out of an hourly rate of £10.50, I would have to pay less than the minimum wage to cover the sick pay plus a cover worker. The alternative is that I take time off work to cover the absent shifts but as I said above, I wouldn't have any income and I can't imagine qualifying for any benefit under those circumstances – I'm not sick. I can't sign on as I'm fit for work and not unemployed. ATOS would have a field day with a claim like that.

For a long time, I've wanted to transfer the whole support package over to the care agency that provides the rest of Steven's support. The council won't agree to that, purely on financial grounds. As I said, the direct payment hourly rate is £10.50 per hour; the agency rate is £16.85 per hour. It would cost the council nearly 50% more and they'll never go for that. And neither will the support staff. Out of the £10.50 I receive from the LA, I can pay them £9 per hour (which still covers holiday pay and a small amount of sick pay). Although the agency receives £16.85 from the council, their pay their employees, on average, £7.50 per hour. They're not interested in negotiating that figure up; it would bite into their 100% profit margin. And the direct payment workers are hardly likely to be keen to transfer their hours the agency and earn £1.50 per hour less.

I'm meant to be going to a mate's wedding in two week's time. As it is in Kent, it will mean at least one, probably two nights away. I'm really looking forward to it because another good friend lives nearby, so I was planning to kill two birds with one stone and spend some time with my two closest friends. I have been saving up my earnings as it will mean losing two days pay. I have also saved up some support hours to cover the extra support that will be needed at home whilst I'm away. Now I will have to cancel as there is no way I can afford to pay someone their week's sick pay; cover for the sick person's normal shifts and cover for the extra two shifts I would need to cover my absence. My mate, the bridegroom , and I have a running joke about our "bitterness" levels. I can well and truly trump him with this one!

Caring is fucking hard. Normal day-to-day stuff takes up an enormous amount of energy. I'm not interested in running a staff; I don't have the time or the energy for that. Has the nature of being a carer become so complicated and involved now that opting out of being an employer, would actually mean forgoing a care package. Carers have enough on their plate – we don't want to have the hassle of being employers as well.

Trussed Up With Trust

August 17, 2012

Every now and then, something happens that feels like a slap around the face with a large soggy moggy. It's the recognition of the enormous amount of trust I have to place in so many people. It's one of the biggest trusts I can ever imagine giving – the trust in keeping my son safe; protecting him from an often hostile world and from his own vulnerability. It can't be done of course but that doesn't stop my trying and investing so much energy and love in the pursuit of his protection. Fortunately, my natural instinct has always been to trust and I'm prepared to accept the hurt that accompanies those times when my trust is abused. I also know that when my trust has been broken, I can be quite brutally ruthless and will want that person's guts for garters. I will never trust Hillingdon council again. I've received the official apology (albeit a mealy-mouthed one) and have had to find a way of working with them cooperatively. But I can never forget that the director of social care authorised a press release the day before the hearing which had the sole purpose of presenting Steven in the worst possible light. I will never forget the judge, on being shown the press release, throwing his hands up in the air and despairing: "This is about a vulnerable man in their care".

But that is raking over old, hot coals that I cannot change. Trust, or the breach of my trust has surfaced again big time this week, as one of Steven's longest-serving support workers has been "let go". I've had a few days of beating myself up that I wasn't brave enough to act sooner and also had to deal with the embarrassment of how much I'd been played by the worker over the weeks.

To grasp how powerful this need to protect is, one has to understand that to Steven, like the majority of people with autism, the world can be a frightening, anxiety provoking place. To be at the mercy of situation after situation that you cannot make sense of must be terrifying. So, to protect himself from this terror, Steven constructs and relies on routines. Hundreds and thousands of routines; some of them sadly unrealistic. And if any of these routines get broken, the fragile shield cracks and the naked vulnerability of this strapping man is exposed. It is unbearable to observe; as I guess it is as unbearable to feel. So, I set myself the impossible task of trying to maintain all the routines. Some are easy: I can always find a shop that will have some lamb chops, so the Saturday tea routine is intact. I can rely on the fact that the lyrics and the video of Take That singing "Relight My Fire" is never going to change. Some of the verbal routines are harder; they require me to have instant access to a catalogue of scripts stored in my brain. Sometimes, if I'm tired, my search function lets me down and that can have hairy consequences. (You'd think I'd know after several hundred viewings the follow on line to Sybil Fawlty's "Burst his zip today Andre"). It gets even hairier when the reliance on the routine depends on other external sources; from a character taking a break from a soap opera, to one of Steven's friends at the Mencap pool remembering that Steven likes to serenade him with "Heartbeat" as they greet each other.

The other thing that presses all my buttons is when people use Steven and his condition to cover up their own stuff; their own indiscretions. It happened all the time at the positive behaviour unit. Take the incident that led to the council issuing the first deprivation of liberty authorisation when Steven escaped from the unit. There has never been any acknowledgement that they failed in their duty of care that day. Worse, they used the incident as a cover for their real agenda which was to move Steven away. I can't tell you what a relief it was when Justice Peter Jackson saw straight through that manipulation.

That brings me back to the latest dent in my trust this week. Three weeks ago, Steven went out for his normal Thursday afternoon train ride with his two support workers. It's the same routine every week; a trip from one end of the Metropolitan Line to the other, getting out at Aldgate for a bag of salt and vinegar crisps. He loves it. I got home from work that Thursday afternoon and there was nothing untoward reported. The following Monday one of the support workers approached me and told me that he was very uncomfortable about the actions of the other support worker during the train ride. His story was that they had to change trains, Steven became agitated by the change to routine and the second support worker put them all in a dangerous situation. He convinced me to cancel the train journey for the duration of the Olympics as he felt it would put too much pressure on everybody. The focus of the conversation though was Steven's behaviour during the trip. As the days passed, I became more and more disconcerted that the second support worker wasn't mentioning the incident. Eventually, I showed him the other guy's report and he got very upset. The reason that he hadn't reported anything was because there hadn't been anything to report. Yes, Steven had become anxious but he felt that any potential problem was contained. He pointed out that the reason the whole situation came about was that the first support worker wanted to leave work early that day and wanted to cut short the journey. Sod the routine. Sod Steven's distress. He wanted to leave early but didn't have the balls to ask. And just like the DoL story at the positive behaviour unit, he tried to use Steven's response to cover up what really happened. I can't be doing with that.

What links Hillingdon and this support worker in their arrogance is that they totally overlook that the truth usually comes out – from Steven himself. He doesn't understand the concept of a lie and in his own idiosyncratic way will find a way of communicating the truth. A few months after Steven returned home from the positive behaviour unit, he suddenly said to me one night: "Steven Neary's feet got all muddy". The ensuing story consisted of six sentences but told the whole story. After his several escapes from the unit, the staff decided to lock his shoes away in a cupboard in the hall. He had to ask for his shoes whenever he went out. It appears that on this particular day, one of the unit staff was a nasty wanker, who for the sake of argument we'll call "Nick". This was Steven's six sentence story:

"Steven Neary's shoes was in the garden".

"Steven Neary went on the muddy grass".

"Nick threw Steven Neary's shoes outside in the raining"

"Nick was laughing"

"Steven Neary got his shoes back"

"Steven Neary's happy now".

It cuts me up recounting that story but I hope it illustrates that my capacity to trust is constantly on a knife-edge. That chap was always very agreeable whenever I met him. There would have been absolutely no point in making a complaint because in all likelihood it would have led to Steven being abused further. I don't mean in further incidents like that; Steven was at home by now anyway. No, for me, it's as big an abuse to deny him his version of his reality and to have his vulnerability turned on its head, so that he becomes the problem.

Thank goodness that I have several people around me that I trust completely. Without them, the terror of how easily Steven's vulnerability can put him in danger would be quite unbearable.

Ground Control To HMRC

February 26, 2013

Has anyone tried to contact the HMRC recently? Verbally? One human voice to another? It's a dying art.

I've been self employed since 1999. I religiously complete my self assessment each year on time and I've never once been late with the two payments in June and December. I'm not sure where my fear of the taxman comes from but it's akin to the terrible anxiety I used to feel whenever I spotted one of the security guards prowling the aisles in Woolworths. I immediately assumed a look of pure guilt and would find myself looking over my shoulder as I searched the shelves for the latest Rubettes' album.

I suspected something was amiss when my bill for the second half year's tax didn't arrive in December. I phoned HMRC twice: one call took 35 minutes; the other 50 minutes. On neither occasion did I speak to a fellow human. Instead I was passed from one collection of press keypad options to another. So, I wrote to them, asking what has happened to my bill. Probably crossing in the post (I've never known HMRC act so speedily), I received a letter two days letter informing me that as I hadn't submitted my self assessment back in April, I was now liable for a fine. Anticipating a long prison stretch, I immediately wrote back, enclosing my accounts for the previous financial year. And then – nothing.

On 5th January, I received another letter, thanking me fro my letter and notifying me that Mrs Huffer, had contacted the self assessment section and they would be forwarding me a new self assessment form in the post. Mrs Huffer reminded me that I had until just 31st January to return the form or incur a further penalty. Cue another phone call from me (42 minutes – no human) to ask why they don't assess my tax on the information I've provided.

Needless to say, I didn't hear another word from them until 31st January when the self assessment arrived in the post. It was dated the 17th January. How had it taken over 2 weeks to get to me? I filled it out immediately and had to pay one of Steven's support worker's half an hour overtime whilst I flew down to the post office to send it off.

On 4th February, I received a very threatening letter, scolding me for still not returning my self assessment form and reminding me that both my payment of tax and the fine was now overdue. I tossed off a nervy but angry reply. All I wanted was a fucking bill.

On Saturday, 23rd, I received a letter telling me that my tax for the last year had been calculated and quoting the two half yearly figures (very much less than last year!). But no bill. I know it was Saturday but HMRC are meant to be open to 4pm, so I tried to phone them again. 1 hour and 5 minutes later, a female machine said to me: "There's a lot of people waiting to speak to an agent. Goodbye".

I'd like to say "goodbye" too but would probably have my fine quadrupled and be made to eat three dozen hard boiled eggs without a drink. Apart from my pen pal, Mrs Huffer, who may or may not exist, I've spent over 6 hours trying to speak to someone at HMRC and haven't had the joy of speaking to a fellow human yet.

The Public Ear & the State Eye

January 30, 2013

I read two interesting things yesterday that led me to reflect on my relationship with social media and the wider media. The first was a tweet from @sarsiobhan that she had received a negative comment on her blog. The comment was critical of her writing about her son and bringing his life into the public domain. The second was a discussion at @SWCmedia on exactly the same topic; is it right for family members to write about their vulnerable children, particularly on the internet? The general view was that it was not a good thing and seldom in the vulnerable person's best interests and the lack of control of how the material is received could put the person at risk. Familiar concepts in the social care world: control, best interests and risk. So much social care discourse and actions are framed in these terms and the drive to avoid risk often wins the day.

In my case, I brought Steven's situation in 2010 to the media out of sheer desperation. After six months of having his access to justice blocked by Hillingdon council, he needed more help than I could give him to secure his release from the deprivation of his liberty. I was confident that I could shield him from any negative attention; I wasn't totally sure of course but it seemed worth the risk. And it worked. It was through the Facebook campaign and Twitter connections that we eventually got legal representation. And I was able to gain valuable knowledge about DoLs that had been denied me by the supervisory body. In the court judgement, the team manager is quoted as saying that the media attention did push Hillingdon to reflect on their decision-making; albeit that it didn't change anything. I don't think it's an exaggeration to say that without social media and the involvement of the press, Steven would today be languishing in a hospital in Wales. Facing a life in care that does not want or does not need.

That was then. What about now? Since the court case, the Get Steven Home group continues to be a vibrant group and the pool of knowledge there helps an awful lot of people. It's very difficult to get appropriate help; have your voice heard when you're in the sort of threatening situations that the social care world throws up. People come into the group on a daily basis with harrowing stories of powerlessness and are caught up in horrendous battles with the authorities. This isn't a Jeremy Kyle culture of washing dirty linen in public (as someone put it on SWCmedia last night). This is about despair and survival. Following 2010, I wrote the book and that certainly involved more disclosure than had been in the public domain up to that point. From the feedback I've received, I know that the book is on the reading list on several professional courses, so that can only be a good thing. And I write this blog; partly because I love writing but also because I believe there are important stories still to tell. I see my blog as similar to Sara Ryan's in that they are both about the narrative of trying to lead a "normal" family life whilst being entrapped in systems that claim to be about support. I also believe that both Sara and I write with a great deal of love and humour and a deep understanding of the people we care for that nor professional could ever have. I like to think in our writing, Steven and LB come alive and their wit, humanness and struggles come across. Compare my writing about Steven with the press release that Hillingdon issued on the eve of the court case and then argue about who has his best interests at heart and which could cause him most harm.

I'm always uneasy by the opinion that the professional's view of best interests carries more weight that the families' view because the professional is able to take a more detached position. Whilst they won't have the same emotional investment as the family; they are hardly entering the arena with a completely clean agenda. They may be detached from the person but I doubt they can be detached from all the other agendas (money, resources, local politics) that come into play. I often find that professionals will imagine worst case scenarios and build their position from that. Understandable perhaps but no way to live a fulfilling life because the position will be not to do something rather than do something and try to minimise the risks involved.

In an evidence reliant world, the evidence in our case reveals that there has been absolutely no adverse impact on Steven that we have encountered from the media attention or from my writing about our story. I say, "We have encountered" because there may be some saddo having a wank over a picture of me on the steps of the High Court but I can't get too worked up about it if I don't know about it. Steven will occasionally ask to see the BBC news footage but to him, they are part of his video collection alongside his school plays and the person centred plan footage of him at the gym. Steven remembers the names of the journalists and they've been added to his portfolio of lookalikes. And every now and then a member of the public recognises him, introduces themselves and congratulates him. Which makes him very happy. That's it. No doorstepping. No hostile public reaction. No nasty anonymous letters. I haven't dropped my protectiveness but in three years there have been no unwanted attention for Steven to deal with.

Last week, I spoke at a BIA conference and I had a few random negative thoughts beforehand: "should I put the story to bed now?", "Does it benefit Steven from me attending these events?", "Does telling the story serve any useful purpose?" The response I received was incredible. People were moved. People said they were inspired. But perhaps most importantly, a number of delegates told me that our case had prompted them to examine their practice. That must be a good thing.

Not everyone, even in 2013, is an X Factor wannabe. If your priorities are right; if your heart is in the right place; if you explore your unconscious motives; if you are confident of protecting your vulnerable relative, it is important to tell your story and for your story to be heard,

Sometimes we have to stand up and be counted.

Got Steven Home

2010 was all about Getting Steven home and giving him the life that he wants to live. This final section, is a series of pieces about normal life at home with Steven:

- That Old Familiar December Feeling
- Olivia Newton John & Positive Behaviour
- I Don't Want A Horse
- It's Only A Sodding DoL's Conference
- Afternoon Tea With Coolio
- The Price of Trauma
- Why Risk Assessments Are So Risky

That Old Familiar December Feeling

December 28, 2012

And so it has started. It happened at this time last year and yesterday saw the start of this year's late December traumatic anxiety surfacing for Steven. December is always a difficult time for Steven because being autistic, his normal routines are the foundation stones of his life and his piece of mind and in December they are severely disrupted. The anxiety starts as soon as Countdown goes off the air in the second week in December; it is the first of the routines being dismantled. Then for three days from Christmas Eve to Boxing Day a calm descends because the yearly routine of these three days is that there is no routine which is a routine in itself. These days certainly don't have the same routine as the other 362 days. Since Steven returned home on Christmas Eve 2010, we now have a new, overwhelming anxiety that will grip from 27th December and probably last until Countdown returns on 7th January.

Last night we went to bed just before 10pm. Between 10 and 11, Steven called me into his room 17 times, seeking reassurance that he's "not going back to M House for a massive break next Wednesday" (It was a Wednesday that he went away in 2009. It's not surprising that for someone who remembers that he ate jelly tots on the train on a Thursday in 1996, that he remembers the significance of this particular Wednesday). At 12.30, I was woken by the sound of him sobbing and sat on his bed for half an hour. He was pleading with me to "stay in the Uxbridge house with Dad forever and ever". This lasted until 1.15 when he fell asleep. At 2.30am, he came rushing into my bedroom, grabbed my arm and nearly pulled me out of bed in his desperation – "Dad's not putting Steven's clothes in the bag for a break?" I showed him the empty suitcase and his clothes hanging in his wardrobe but it took until 3.15 before he calmed down and went back to bed. At 4.30. I was awoken again by Steven screaming. This time it was a combination of "not going to M House after Christmas" and "want to stay with Mark Neary all days". This lasted until 5.15, during which time, Steven became so agitated he wet himself. Neither of us was able to get back to sleep and at 6am the support worker arrived to take charge of the morning bath. Steven manfully got on with his Friday routine of watching a Men Behaving Badly DVD; I got on with my Friday routine of the weekly Sainsbury's shop at 7am and work at 10am. Later, Steven refused to get out of the car when they got to his Friday day centre because the manager of the positive behaviour unit goes there and "don't want Dave (name change) to take Steven to M House".

Let's not talk about social stories, picture charts and behaviour logs – they don't even touch the sides when we're talking this degree of trauma. There is no point in seeking the input from the professionals involved in Steven's care – they are not allowed to acknowledge how traumatized Steven has been because that (in their eyes) infers liability and that is the thing that matters the most. I don't give a fuck about liability; I just want a good night's sleep for the both of us. Whilst I am sitting with Steven, comforting and reassuring him, I am able to bracket off my feelings. Once he is asleep and I am back in my bed, bracketing becomes impossible and the deep sadness of seeing my son so distressed overwhelms me. Despite the obvious drive to avoid any sense of responsibility for their actions, I don't understand the professional's position about the trauma. Whenever I have raised the issue over the past year, the attitude I've received is of dissmissiveness - they haven't witnessed it, so I must be exaggerating. But of course, despite everything that happened in 2010, I am still the person that Steven trusts the most; communicates his most frightening anxieties to, so obviously I'm the person who is going to get the full extent of his December anxiety. Basic psychology - we reveal the most to the people we trust the most. I guess it reveals the enormous chasm within the social care system – where the need to protect the service leads to the denial of the service user's most basic, natural human experience.

In the midst of all this, yesterday I received Hillingdon's bundle that they've submitted to the first tier tribunal for the Housing Benefit appeal. I need to write a response statement but it's hard to find the time or motivation when you're drying a pissed mattress. I'd quite like to watch my new "Dark Knight Rises" DVD before I give attention to a Housing Benefit appeal, that is, like the DoL of 2010, a complete sham – a state decision used as a cover for a more unseemly action.

Post deprivation of liberty trauma; a vacuous housing benefit appeal; Batman. Happy New Year. We had a fantastic time on Boxing Day. Steven, me and two of the support workers went to Hampton open air swimming pool (incidentally, one of the things rejected on Steven's person centred plan wish list for being too dangerous). We swam. We froze. We whizzed down the water slide. We sang The Beautiful South songs underwater. We felt alive for two hours. Social care systems can kill the soul; they have nothing to do with living. And how on earth do we begin to address that tragedy?

Olivia Newton John & Positive Behaviour

January 6, 2013

Amongst Steven's Christmas present wish list was "a Olivia Newton John CD with all the songs on". So, I duly brought her greatest hits and this afternoon Steven wanted to play it through for the first time. He has been humming a song for a few days and trying to get me to name it but it drew a blank with me.

So, we arrive at "Take Me Home – Country Roads" and he gets all excited and tells me that this was another song he used to sing to the staff at the positive behaviour unit as a way of trying to convey the message that he wanted to "come home to the Uxbridge house".

It made me realise again that Steven must have had a whole playlist of songs that he would break into at the positive behaviour unit, in an attempt to be heard. Anyone who knows Steven knows that he communicates best through song and that our daily conversation can get quite operatic at times. It doesn't take a genius to register that is how he likes to communicate and to try to understand the message of the song.

Another area for the mental capacity assessment to be extended to cover all aspects of communicating perhaps?

I Don't Want A Horse

February 17, 2013

On Friday, I received the cheque for Steven's damages award. I defy anyone who receives an unexpected lump sum not to consider a treat. This is how the conversation went:

Me: "Steve – would you like a big surprise for your birthday?" (I knew this was too vague a question)

Steve: "A BIG surprise? A BIG one? I don't want a horse".

Me: "No, not a horse. Would you like a special treat? Do you want to go and see a show?"

Steve: "Seen Grease. Seen Blood Brothers. No, not a show"

Me: "Would you like to go on a holiday for your birthday?"

Steve: (laughing) A holiday in March. Dad's doing silly talking.

Me: "No. We can have a birthday holiday and a summer holiday"

Steve: "That's a bit greedy. Center Parcs in March?"

Me: "We can go to Center Parcs in March. Shall we go to Center Parcs in March?"

Steve: (Getting very excited) Yes. Phone Uncle Wayne and tell him we're going to Center Parcs".

So, Center Parcs it is then. This was one of the things on Steven's person centred plan wish list in 2010 that was refused by the positive behaviour unit. He's always wanted to go there since he was about seven and saw pictures of his two cousins there. But if we go, there might be a problem:

Worse Case Scenario:

I lose my housing benefit appeal and the Local Authority decide to pursue their suggestion to apply to the court to be appointed decision maker on where he should live. They decide to make Steven the tenant but won't offer him social housing as his capital exceeds their limit for social housing. They decide that I have deliberately disposed of some capital in order to obtain the best outcome for Steven and refuse housing. That may sound paranoid but this is Hillingdon we're talking about.

Center Parcs is quite expensive at about £1200 for the week. And we'd have to take two support workers with us and they would have to be paid for 24 hour shifts as they are away from home (which is fair enough). And we'd have to hire a car to get us there and back. But as they say on Deal or No Deal – "this is a once in a lifetime experience", so what the hell. If it causes problems at a later date, we'll cross that bridge when we come to it. I cannot imagine any reasonable person disagreeing with the trip after what Steven has been through.

And as he says, he doesn't want a horse. He did double check though that going on a holiday for his birthday wouldn't compromise him getting a new Robson and Jerome CD. Got to get the priorities right.

It's Only A Bloody DoL's Conference

February 26, 2013

On Friday 1st March, I've been invited back to speak at the Yorkshire and Humber DoL's Conference. In fact, I have an afternoon session entitled "A Q&A with Mark Neary". I like that – it puts me in mind of An Audience with Dame Edna Everage". I might end my Q&A by lobbing gladioli into the audience. It's an honour to be invited and I'm really looking forward to it. Since becoming a Leeds United supporter, me and Leeds are old flames now. This time, I'm going to forsake the claustrophobic attention of Jefferson, the Maitre D at the Premier Inn; I'm going to pass up a revisit to the noxious smell in the bathroom at the Park Plaza. Instead I'm parking up at the Crowne Plaza. I'll get there just after 5pm; perhaps half an hour in the spa pool; a hearty meal and then a couple of drinks in the bar whilst reading the latest Socrates novel. Just what Dr Feelgood ordered.

But my goodness, the preparation for it is a military operation. I did the weekly shopping today (instead of Friday). Tomorrow, I've got the meeting about my housing benefit in the morning and then work from 2pm to 8pm, so couldn't do the shopping then. By the times I get home tomorrow night, the support worker will be clocking off, so won't have time for anything then.

I've got an hour tomorrow morning to:

Pack
Sort out Steven's medication for two days.
Write my talk.
Label up 20 music DVDs for the support worker to do the Thursday night DVD session
Sort out the meals for two days.
Sort changes of clothes for 2 days
Rewind 2 videos so they are cued up for the Christmas Top of The Pops music session on Friday morning.
Plait my pubic hair.

If ever I meet someone and they suggest a romantic weekend in Paris, I'll need two week's notice for the arrangements.

Afternoon Tea With Coolio

March 5, 2013

I heard Steven chatting to his support worker whilst he was in the bath this morning – "Steven Neary's got a very busy hard work today".

And he was right. This was his gruelling day:

- Watched an episode from the 1993 quarter finals of Gladiators.

- Off to Virgin Active for his water aerobics and spa pool.

- Changed the sheets on his bed.

- Did a compilation music tape that he's been planning since the weekend. "Going to have Coolio and Bucks Fizz".

- Watched the Fawlty Towers episode with Mr O'Reilly, the builder. Running commentary throughout.

- Over an hour and half on the computer looking for clips of Moby.

- Catalogued the photos of his grandmother by dress colour.

Interestingly, he didn't include loading up the washing machine and doing the washing up as part of his hard work day.

As he got out of the cab after swimming, the driver asked Steven what he had planned for the afternoon:

"It's a big busy. Got Coolio. It's a marvellous musical montage".

The Price of Trauma

March 15, 2013

I've had a bit of a change of heart after the last three nights. Ever since the court case, I've always been very uneasy on the subject of damages. I loathe the compensation culture that exists in this country. I let the Official Solicitor pursue the subject of Steven's damages and tried not to get involved. I went against advice from my barrister and didn't pursue any damages for myself. And since Steven received them three weeks ago, and the whole housing situation and the manipulative way Hillingdon are treating his damages, I've actually been thinking about giving them back. The damages are proving more trouble than they're worth.

However, the last three nights have been awful. Steven has had no more than four hours sleep each night since Tuesday; I've probably had about three hours. He's been waking up about 11pm, in a terrible state of upset and anxiety. This morning at 1.30, it all came out.

On Fridays Steven goes to a day centre. It is run by the positive behaviour team and Steven often bumps into the manager there. We'll call him John Green, for the sake of argument. This is the same man who in 2010, cancelled Steven's holiday to Somerset two weeks before we were due to go as the positive behaviour team had decided Steven was too great a risk to be unleashed on the good folks of Burnham on Sea.

So, I'm sitting on Steven's bed as he's trying to rip his duvet up and he's sobbing. Eventually, he grabbed me in a bear hug and said he didn't want to go to the day centre today. I kept reassuring him that he didn't have to go if he didn't want to and then after an almighty sob and scream he shouted: "Don't want John Green tell Steven Neary can't go to Center Parcs".

I spent two hours reassuring him that we ARE GOING to Center Parcs and nobody is going to stop us and eventually he fell asleep at 3am.

I got back to bed but haven't slept for the many thoughts running round my head. One of the worst is the question; when will the trauma ever end for him? Has it now mapped out a life for him of distrust and uncertainty? No matter how much he trusts me, Steven has learned that Dad can be trumped. There are people more powerful than Dad who can make huge decisions in his life. Even if we plan something together (and the trunks, birthday presents and snacks have been in the bag for over a week, Steven is checking the bag at least 10 times a day), he knows that someone can come along and change all those plans. I don't see an end to that.

I am raging. I keep thinking of all those pointless meetings over the last three years with the in-house psychologist and the positive behaviour team and the amount of energy they have put into denying that Steven has suffered any lasting effects of 2010. They couldn't give a toss about him; it's all about accountability. But if they acknowledge that, the damages may have been higher. Money drives again.

I can manage the next three days. I'm expecting the next three nights to be the same and Steven's distress will only abate when we're on the road on Monday morning.

But it will be temporary. There will be something else that is important to him. Something else that will cause great anxiety because he'll be terrified that it will be taken from him again.

Why Risk Assessments Are So Risky

March 23, 2013

We've just got back from a week's break at Center Parcs. It was a wonderful experience. There was me, Steven and two of his support workers. We had an "exclusive executive villa", which meant we had our own spa pool, steam room and games room. Four bedrooms, each with their own en-suite facilities (bath, toilet, a grazing yak). Too bad that we had the villa at the furthest point of the site, meaning a good 35 minute walk to any of the facilities. We needed the exercise and by crikey, we got it. By the third day, Steven was flagging and he wanted a day in. So, we just had two two-hour sessions in the spa pool, with his new Muriel's Wedding Soundtrack CD serenading our bubbling.

The support workers were fantastic – they wouldn't let me lift a finger. They took charge of night-times, so for the first time in about two years, I had some unbroken night's sleep. I can't tell you how strange it feels to wake up feeling sprightly, having had seven hours un-interrupted sleep. I also observed the support workers as we were going about our business on the park (or accessing the parc community). They know exactly what to do when faced with situations that Steven might find anxiety provoking. He's always troubled by screaming babies and in order to enter the Subterranean Water Paradise, we had to walk through the "Buggy Bay" – literally over a hundred buggies parked, of course alerting us to the possibility that they were probably going to be over a hundred toddlers inside the Subterranean Water Paradise. And there were.

Of course, if Steven had still been in the positive behaviour unit, he wouldn't have got beyond the buggy park. In fact, he probably wouldn't have even been allowed to set foot in the whole park. On their assessment scale model, a buggy park would have scored "an intolerable risk". End of activity. He wouldn't have been allowed to do his favourite holiday activity; going down the water slides and flumes because the risk assessment would have considered the possibility of a meltdown at the top of the flume, putting others at risk. He wouldn't have been allowed to go out for a meal at the wonderful Forresters Inn – they served their drinks in glasses (not plastic beakers) and glasses would have been classified as a potential weapon. The village shop would have been out of bounds – too confined a space. A walk around the lake would have been out of the question – Steven might have decided to run into the lake and he is too big and strong for anyone to stop him. And climbing up two steps (slippery ones!) to get into the spa pool would ahve been a complete no-no.

If you think I'm exaggerating, one day I'll post a copy of one of Steven's many risk assessments and you'll see that no stone is left unturned in assessing the risk of Steven living a life.

Needless to say, nothing untoward happened. Myself and the support workers know that if we are walking along a footpath and a howling baby starts coming in the opposite direction, you engage Steven in an in-depth conversation about Take That and he doesn't even notice the child. He's not going to have a meltdown on the wild water rapids because he is too busy singing "Yes Sir, I Can Boogie" in his excitement. Etc etc etc.

But when everything is assessed so microscopically for its potential risk, of course a risk is going to be found. Thankfully, I'm prepared to take the risk of finding a grazing yak on my personal snooker table and being subsequently head butted by said yak. And in the process, Steven might just have a life worth living.

Finale

Thanks to everyone who has supported me and Steven since 2010.

If you can't beat them, join them:

- Of All The Job Interviews In All The World

Of All the Job Interviews, In All The World

March 13, 2013

A friend of mine sent me the link to a job advert on Hillingdon Council's website. It is for a "Positive Behaviour Manager – Children's Services" and is actually based at the same place where Steven was held in 2010. My mate dared me to apply for the job. So here, with minimal fabrication, is a transcript of my interview with Deidre Tressell – Deputy Director of Person Centred Transformation (South):

Deidre: Welcome Mr Neary. First of all, can you tell us what experience you've had of dealing with challenging behaviour?

Me: Well….. I had to deal with you kidnapping my son for a year. That was pretty challenging.

Deidre: Ooops. My bad. Never mind. Lessons have been learned. Lines have been drawn. Bla bla bla. And how would you work with a child displaying inappropriately challenging behaviour?

Me: I'd congratulate them on being able to communicate their feelings. And then I'd make sure that all the people involved in working with them were trained in tuning in and relating to the person.

Deidre: So, your emphasis would be on the professionals, rather than the service user?

Me: All the time. They're the ones finding the behaviour challenging after all. Seems a good place to start.

Deidre: A novel idea Mr Neary but self reflection is not our modus operandi. At Hillingdon, we have a proven track record using a model where every aspect of the service user's life is broken down. The goal is to take away every coping mechanism they have and rebuild them the Hillingdon way.

Me: Sounds intriguing. Does it work?

Deidre: Every time. They completely collapse. And we meticulously log their breakdown and use it as evidence to send them to a permanent placement, usually many miles away.

Me: And some other schmuck authority will pick up the bill for their care?

Deidre: Exactly. You've been doing your homework Mr Neary. You've been reading our policies. We call that one a transformation pathway.

Me: And my job will be to nudge people along that pathway?

Deidre: In the best person centered way of course. Talking of which, how would you empower the service user by facilitating their person centred plan?

Me: I guess I'd start by asking them what they'd like to do. What they want from their life......

Deidre: Oooh, risky. You may end up having to say "no" to everything they ask for. Try again..

Me: Perhaps I could suggest to them it would promote their independence better than instead of going to the gym, which they have asked to do, they could stay in the residential unit and watch re-runs of Hetty Wainthrop Investigates. It would also give the staff more time on Facebook too.

Deidre. Excellent. We encourage creative person centred planning like that. The service user has to realise that they have many choices we can empower them with.

Me: Thank goodness there are so many television channels these days.

Deidre: Let's get on to the main part of the job specification. At a conservative estimate, 95% of your time will be spent compiling in depth risk assessments and writing risk management plans. Can you meet that criteria Mr Neary?

Me: I suppose my ideas on risk may be considered a bit radical. I like the quote that all life carries risk and what's the point of making someone safe, if they only end up miserable.

Deidre: Sounds like the wooly theory of someone with no knowledge of extreme challenging behaviour.

Me: It was a High Court judge actually.

Deidre: We find our assessment processes extremely successful. If they're thorough enough, we can practically prevent someone doing anything. Think of the cost savings in that. Remove all quality of life and contain them; that way you get plenty of raw data about their challenging behaviour. That's what we're here for.

Me: Yes, I can see that but what about DoLs in those cases?

Deidre: Dolls are playthings Mr Neary – we encourage more worthwhile pursuits. Where do you stand on social stories? Do they have a place in promoting self directed support, whilst underpinning the risk management plan?

Me: I'm getting the hang of this now. You could have a story called: "Mopping The Floor Of My Residential Unit Is Great". That point would need to be repeatedly emphasised until the client was brainwas...., erm, receptive to the idea. Perhaps, for balance, we could have a few pages like; "Going to the cinema is bad because I might choke on some popcorn". That sort of thing.

Deidre: Super. We'll introduce you to the speech therapist. You'll get on like a house on fire. Good care costs Mr. Neary, in these austere times, how can we manage that?

Me: Ummm. Provide cheap bad care? Or no care?

Deidre: Good Lord no. No, the answer is to get them to pay through the nose for their care. That's the beauty of personal budgets and the fairer charging policy. We give with one hand and grab straight back with the other. Perfectly equitable.

Me: More to go round then? For all the service users?

Deidre: Well there's more to go round but we can't have the users exhausting the piggybank. Since the introduction of personalisation, the management team has grown fivefold. Get a carer to agree their indicative budget and it's a healthy bonus for the whole team.

Me: I bet you sing a daily hymn to the RAS.

Deidre: One final question. Do you believe there should be specific measures in place to work with the challenging behaviour of someone with autism? And is there a case for shitloads of anti-psychotics in their care plan?

Me: I know this one. I'd write a 36 page report without any reference to autism whatever and conclude with the learned wisdom: "If you know 1 person with autism, then you know 1 person with autism".

Deidre: Shake my hand Mr Neary. I can see you feeling quite at home here.

I start next Tuesday after my two hour training course: "Everything you ever need to know about the Human Rights Act, The Mental Capacity Act and the Deprivation of Liberty Safeguards"

Printed in Great Britain
by Amazon